Leckie × Leckie
Scotland's leading educational publishers

Active LEARNING
Curriculum for Excellence

S1
ENGLISH
Course Notes

2B OR NOT 2B?

David Cockburn

CONTENTS

Introduction 4

TOOLS FOR WRITING

Grammar and sentence structure 6
Nouns 8
Verbs 10
Tenses: present tense 12
Tenses: past tense 14
Tenses: future tense 16
Adjectives 18
Punctuation 20
Spelling 22

CREATING TEXTS

Why do we write? 24
More about register 26
Essay writing 28
Structure: making an essay plan 30
Example: parodies 32

READING FOR UNDERSTANDING

Introduction to reading skills 34
Identifying purpose 36
Finding and using information from texts 38
Reading accurately 40
Making inferences from texts 42
Comparing texts 44
Persuasion 46
Reliability 48

2

READING FOR ENJOYMENT

Introduction	50
Genre	52
Theme	54
Structure: time	56
Structure: point of view – first person narrator	58
Structure: point of view – third person narrator	60
Characterisation	62
Setting	64
Plot	66
Personal response to reading	68

TOOLS FOR LISTENING AND TALKING

Group discussions	70
Note taking	72
Preparing for group discussions	74
Preparing for an individual talk	76
Presenting an individual talk	78

3

ABOUT THE ACTIVE LEARNING SERIES

Leckie & Leckie's Active Learning series has been developed specifically to help teachers, students and parents implement A Curriculum for Excellence as effectively as possible. Each book is subject-based, written for a specific year group and follows the Outcomes and Experiences, at a level appropriate for that year group. For every subject, both a Course Notes book and a Activity Workbook have been published.

These highly innovative books complement existing class textbooks. They address the Curriculum for Excellence in a thoroughly practical way that makes learning both engaging and fun! A summary of each topic is included before going on to focus on ideas for activities and rich tasks, bringing the topic to life. In line with the principles and philosophies of Curriculum for Excellence, every Course Notes book provides creative ideas for making cross-disciplinary links with other classroom subjects, and, crucially, illustrates the relevance of each topic to everyday life.

The Activity Workbooks present yet more ideas for activities and offer easy to implement suggestions for:

- inter-disciplinary project work,
- topic revision questions,
- an assessment checklist and
- a four capacities mind map.

This ground-breaking new series provides you with a toolkit of ideas, subject links and activities for you to use in the classroom and/or at home.

Leckie & Leckie's Active Learning series - bringing Curriculum for Excellence to life.

LAYOUT OF YOUR COURSE NOTES BOOK

This Course Notes book covers the third level Outcomes and Experiences. These have been organised into chapters, with a different topic covered on each double page spread.

Every double page spread opens with a knowledge summary for a particular topic which conveys key ideas and concepts. The key topic knowledge is enhanced by a practical example, illustration or case study to reinforce learning. A *Top Tip* is also included to highlight key information.

Each double page spread also includes the following features:

Be Active! column. This column lists questions to assess knowledge and understanding and/or activities to be tried in order to deepen understanding of each topic.

Make the Link box. This box highlights the relevance of the topic to a number of other school subjects. This enables learners to gain a more holistic understanding of each topic.

Our Everyday Lives box. This box provides an example of how each topic relates to real life, in order to demonstrate its practical relevance.

Did You Know? box. This box contains an additional fact about each topic to engage further interest and to bring the subject to life.

HOW TO USE YOUR COURSE NOTES BOOK

The Course Notes book sets out to provide teachers and students with a valuable toolkit of easy-to-implement ideas for incorporating the philosophies of Curriculum for Excellence into teaching and learning.

The highlighted links with other subjects, activities ideas and real life examples are the perfect starting point for teachers and students to build upon and develop as they explore ideas around a topic. At Leckie & Leckie, our intention is that this Course Notes book will inspire learners to investigate subjects both widely and deeply in practical and creative ways.

Leckie & Leckie welcome further ideas for the Active Learning series and any feedback that you may have. Please write to us at:

Leckie & Leckie
4 Queen Street
Edinburgh EH2 1JE
Email: enquiries@leckieandleckie.co.uk

GRAMMAR AND SENTENCE STRUCTURE

Learning objectives: to understand the ways in which an English sentence is put together and to learn the various word classes in English especially nouns, verbs and adjectives.

Grammar is the system of rules about the ways in which any language is put together.

Sentence structure

The way you arrange a sentence on a page is decided by the grammar of the language.

You already know that it makes perfect sense to write: *The boy with the broken arm managed to come to my party*.

And that it makes little sense to write: *The managed arm broken boy party my come with the two to*.

> **TOP TIP**
> **Grammar** is the word we use to describe the overall structure of language.
> **Syntax** is the word we use to describe the rules about how an individual sentence is put together.

You can see right away that the order we put the words in gives the sentence its sense. Meaning in an English sentence (unlike many other languages, such as French, German, and Latin) depends on word order and not really on word endings.

Because, in English, meaning depends on the order of the words in any sentence, when you alter the order of the words you also alter the meaning. **Therefore knowing about the rules (called syntax) for word order will help you in your reading and in your writing**.

Word classes

All words in English are classified into their various types. In this book, you will learn about nouns, verbs and adjectives.

However, the classification of words into word classes isn't easy since any given word in English can do many different jobs.

EXAMPLE

Take the word 'square'. It can be a verb, an adjective and a noun.

- She squared up to the girl who had insulted her. (verb)

- I bought a square table yesterday. (adjective)

- The sides of a square have to be of equal length. (noun)

BE ACTIVE

TASK 1

Put the following words into meaningful sentences.

- infection of risk pet don't your leave at
- out carry we tail nose to checks health
- a shop over table coffee cup along a falls
- ken to used that I deid lang they are folk
- Malkies when wee the whit'll come dae ye the
- skate I to to in the learn intend future sometime

TASK 2

How many uses can you find for the word 'draw'? How many uses can you find for the word 'line'?

TASK 3

Can French do the same with words? Let's take the word 'snow' and look at how we use it and how our uses translate into French. Try doing this exercise for the language you are studying.

English	French
snow	la neige
to snow	neiger
snow plough	chasse-neige
snowstorm	tempête de neige
snowdrop	perce-neige
snowball	boule de neige
snowdrift	congère
snowflake	flacon de neige
to be snowed in	bloqué par la neige
to be snowed under	the French do not have this expression

MAKE THE LINK

Not many other languages follow the same sentence structure as English. In **German**, for example, the verb often comes at the end of the sentence. And nouns have to have capital letters – which means that when you're writing German you have to be able to recognise a noun.

Often, in English, the same word has different meanings depending on the context. For example, the word 'product' means one thing when we refer to the products on the supermarket shelves, yet it can mean something quite different when we talk about the product of two numbers. So the word changes in meaning when you go from your **Home Economics** class to your **Maths** class.

DID YOU KNOW?

Sometimes we turn nouns into verbs – for example, take the noun 'London'. There is now a verb 'to be londoned' (note the lower case 'l') which means to be conned, to be ripped off, to pay over the odds for poor service.

OUR EVERYDAY LIVES:

Make a poster for your class notice board. It will be for listing all the words that have recently been made into verbs – for example, 'to goal' as in 'Beckham just goaled that one'. As you come across such words in your everyday lives, they can be added to the poster.

nouns

Learning objectives: to understand the definition of a noun.

A noun is a word which names things. It can be the name of a person, an animal, a place, a thing or a concept. For example, boy, girl, pen, dog, tree, apple, desk, computer, phone, eyebrow, camera, happiness, grief, beauty, John, Inverness, North Sea, Shetland, Elizabeth, Edinburgh Castle, Loch Leven, birth, relationships and death are all nouns.

EXAMPLE

We can classify all these nouns into four types: concrete, abstract, proper and collective.

Concrete noun	Abstract noun	Proper noun	Collective noun
apple	happiness	Kieran	a **pride** of lions
cinema	laughter	Stirling	a **gaggle** of geese
letter	grief	Pentland Firth	a **litter** of pups
cable	love	France	a **troop** of monkeys
banana	manipulation	Ben Nevis	a **covey** of grouse
ear	freedom	Macbeth	a **host** of angels
pen	independence	Loch Leven castle	a **school** of whales
grass	authority	New York	a **skulk** of foxes
cup	loyalty	Prince William	a **conspiracy** of ravens

TOP TIP

Remember that proper nouns are given capital letters, e.g. Kylie, Falkirk, Forth Road Bridge.

BE ACTIVE

TASK 1

Working in small groups, draw a table and then classify the following nouns according to the four classifications: concrete, abstract, proper, collective. Remember to put capital letters in the correct places.

1. yellow
2. boyhood
3. information
4. engine
5. round
6. flock
7. george square
8. herd
9. virgin atlantic
10. plate

TASK 2

Working in pairs, put capital letters in the correct places in the following sentences.

1. i went to asda to do some shopping.
2. the discovery is in dry dock off the river tay.
3. edinburgh is the capital of scotland.
4. one of our greatest actors is sir ian mckellan.
5. the departure lounge at aberdeen airport can be very busy.
6. i have a dog called benson.
7. my sister likes twilight by stephanie meyer.
8. my grandpa laing never misses an episode of river city.

TOOLS FOR WRITING

MAKE THE LINK

When you come across characters in **History** or countries and place names in **Geography**, remember to give them capital letters. For example, Mary, Queen of Scots was born at Linlithgow Palace, Linlithgow, Scotland in 1542 and was executed at Fotheringhay Castle, Northamptonshire, on 7 February 1587.

DID YOU KNOW?

Our vocabulary is always absorbing new words – in the past few years we have seen several new words to do with computers and technology added to English:

- e-commerce,
- e-business,
- e-shopping.

In addition, prefixes, such as 'eco' are now placed in front of words to form new terms:

- ecocide,
- ecosphere.

9

OUR EVERYDAY LIVES:

Look at the following advertisement – note the number of technical words that would have made no sense at all a couple of decades ago.

In Utilities & Operating Systems

Glary Utilities Pro

License:
Free to try;
£39.95 to buy

File size:
4.85 MB

Minimum requirements:
Windows 2000/
XP/Vista

Category:
System Utilities

If you're a home user with low-security issues, it's worth trying this user-friendly toolbox of optimising utilities. Nicely designed with quick performance, Glary Utilities Pro will appeal to less experienced users.

Glary Utilities Pro launches a simply but nicely designed, tabbed interface for performing system cleanup and maintenance. Its basic scan includes a Registry cleaner, shortcuts fixer, startup manager, temporary files cleaner, tracks eraser (activity history and internet traces), and a spyware and adware remover. Determining how to use this utility is very easy, thanks to its clear-cut design and organisation.

VERBS

Learning objectives: to understand the role of verbs in English.

What is a verb? It is quite difficult to answer that question, though the traditional answer is that a verb is a 'doing word' – and most of the time that is as useful an answer as any.

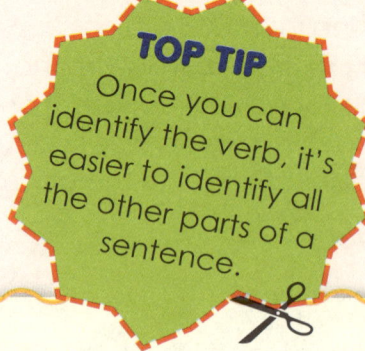

TOP TIP
Once you can identify the verb, it's easier to identify all the other parts of a sentence.

EXAMPLE

Take the following example:

The girl *crossed* the playground.

In the sentence above, the verb is quite definitely the doing word – what did the girl do? – she **crossed** the playground.

But sometimes a verb is not about action: sometimes it is about a state of being or existence.

Take the sentence: My hair *is* brown.

Clearly, my hair isn't **doing** anything – it is just there, it exists. But it **is** still a verb.

10

Look at the following sentences – the verbs have been put into italics for you.

- The boy *clapped* the dog.
- The girl *phoned* her boyfriend.
- Her boyfriend *texted* her back.
- Dominique *is* from Paris.
- Paris *is* the capital of France.
- The river that *flows* through Glasgow is the Clyde.

BE ACTIVE

TASK 1

Now, working in pairs, underline the verbs in the following paragraph from a short story by Roald Dahl.

> The room was warm and clean, the curtains drawn, the two table lamps alight – hers and the one by the empty chair opposite. On the sideboard behind her, two tall glasses, soda water, whisky. Fresh ice cubes in the Thermos bucket.
>
> Mary Maloney was waiting for her husband to come home from work.

What do you notice about the number of verbs in the paragraph? Did you have any difficulties in identifying any of the verbs in the first sentence?

TASK 2

Again, in pairs underline the verbs from this, the first stanza of *To a Mouse* by Robert Burns.

Wee, sleekit, cow'rin, tim'rous beastie,
   O, what a panic's in thy breastie!
Thou need na start awa sae hasty,
   Wi' bickering brattle!
I wad be laith to rin an' chase thee,
   Wi' murd'ring prattle!

MAKE THE LINK

When we make up (or 'coin') a new verb, the chances are that it is a regular verb (see Did You Know?). For example, the verb 'to goal' forms its past tense by adding –ed, as in 'Beckham has just goaled for Manchester'. You may hear this in PE!

It is important to be able to recognise the verb in **Gaelic** – for example, the verb must come first in a sentence, and there are no single words to mean 'yes' or 'no'; instead the main verb is repeated in either its positive or negative form.

DID YOU KNOW?

Verbs are also classified as either **regular** or **irregular**. A regular verb forms its past tense by adding –ed, as in **jump → jumped**, whereas an irregular verb forms its past tense by changing the vowel, as in **swim → swum**. Sometimes a verb is irregular because it doesn't change at all when it forms the past tense, as in **I cast the net → I have cast the net**.

OUR EVERYDAY LIVES:

In spoken English, we sometimes use verb forms that are unacceptable in written English. For example, you hear people say 'I seen' for 'I have seen' and 'I done' for 'I have done'.

Think about how you use verbs and try to note where your spoken language is different from your written language.

TENSES: PRESENT TENSE

Learning objectives: to be able to recognise the present, past, and future tenses, and to understand their functions.

The present tense tells us about what is happening now, and in English you can express the present tense in three different ways. This means that we can make very subtle distinctions when using present time. Take the verb 'to swim' for example: we can say 'I am swimming', meaning that the action is occurring right now, but 'I swim' can mean that I am swimming right now or it can mean that I am a swimmer. We can also emphasise the present tense. For example:

Question: You don't swim, do you?
Answer: I do swim.

Therefore, we can say 'I swim' or 'I am swimming' or 'I do swim'.

EXAMPLES

Here are examples of how we use these three present tenses.

Indefinite present

Person	Singular	Plural
1st	I walk	We walk
2nd	You walk	You walk
3rd	He/she/it is walking	They are walking

Emphatic present

Person	Singular	Plural
1st	I do walk	We do walk
2nd	You do walk	You do walk
3rd	He/she/it does walk	They do walk

Continuous present

Person	Singular	Plural
1st	I am walking	We are walking
2nd	You are walking	You are walking
3rd	He/she/it is walking	They are walking

TOP TIP
Poetry normally uses the present tense, whereas the short story and the novel tend to be in the past tense.

12

BE ACTIVE

TASK 1

Have a look at the poems you have studied recently – or look in any anthology of poetry – to check which tense most poems use.

TASK 2

Working in pairs look carefully at the opening paragraph of the following story – *Kidnapped* by RL Stevenson. Change all the past tenses to the present.

> Mr. Campbell, the minister of Essendean, was waiting for me by the garden gate, good man! He asked me if I had breakfasted; and hearing that I lacked for nothing, he took my hand in both of his and clapped it kindly under his arm.
>
> "Well, Davie, lad," said he, "I will go with you as far as the ford, to set you on the way." And we began to walk forward in silence.
>
> "Are ye sorry to leave Essendean?" said he, after awhile.
>
> "Why, sir," said I, "if I knew where I was going, or what was likely to become of me, I would tell you candidly. Essendean is a good place indeed, and I have been very happy there; but then I have never been anywhere else. My father and mother, since they are both dead, I shall be no nearer to in Essendean than in the Kingdom of Hungary, and, to speak truth, if I thought I had a chance to better myself where I was going I would go with a good will."

Apart from changing the past tense to the appropriate present tense, were there any other changes you had to make?

MAKE THE LINK

In **French**, **Italian** and **German** there is only one way of expressing the present tense.

In **French**, for example, the word for to give is donner. Look at their use of the present tense:

- I give   = je donne
- I am giving = je donne
- I do give   = je donne

The French cannot make, in the present tense, the subtle distinctions in meaning that English speakers can make.

DID YOU KNOW?

You never make mistakes with the present tense! If you're watching Hollyoaks and someone asks you what you are doing, you would answer: 'I'm watching TV'. You would never dream of saying: 'I watch TV' – though a non-native speaker might just say that.

13

OUR EVERYDAY LIVES:

Newspapers often use the present tense in their headlines even although the story refers to something that took place in the past. For example, look at this headline from *The Sunday Mail* on 15 March 2009.

Ice wins at Crufts with a hat trick

What do you think the headline refers to? You need to know what takes place at Crufts (it's a dog show) and what is meant by the expression 'a hat trick' (to win/score three times in a row).

TENSES: PAST TENSE

We use the past tense if we want to express events that happened in the past.

English has a few different ways of using the past tense.

- I walked
- I was walking
- I did walk
- I have walked
- I have been walking
- I had walked
- I had been walking

EXAMPLE

The past tense, as the name suggests, allows us to talk about events that have already taken place. We can use the past tense in different ways to talk about the past.

For example:

- I live in Arbroath.   –   I am at the moment living there.
- I lived in Arbroath for a long time.   –   At some point I lived there.
- I have lived in Arbroath for a long time.   –   And I am still living there.
- I had lived in Arbroath for a long time.   –   But now I live somewhere else.

TOP TIP

Although there are many tenses in English, you should be able to recognise the present, past, and future tenses. Often a question in close reading tests your ability to recognise tense.

14

BE ACTIVE

TASK 1

Here is a story told in the present tense – turn all the present tenses into the past tense.

I am out in the country the other day taking photos, not really paying attention to what else is going on. Suddenly out of the corner of my eye I see this raging bull, and what's worse, it sees me. It gives me a funny look and then scrapes at the ground with its front legs, all aggressive. You can imagine how I feel – I start to run but the bull is faster than me. Fortunately I am near a fence which I leap over, tearing my new jeans in the process...

TASK 2

What's the difference between 'I cooked my mum's tea the other day' and 'I was cooking my mum's tea the other day'? The 'was' form suggests that the activity took place (was taking place?) over a period of time.

Now indicate the difference in meaning of the following sentences.

1. Kylie worked very hard

   and

   Kylie has been working very hard

2. We searched the school for you

   and

   We were searching the school for you

3. I hoped you would go on holiday

   and

   I was hoping you would go on holiday

4. I began to have a feeling of dread

   and

   I had begun to have a feeling of dread

5. Darren broke the window

   and

   Darren has broken the window

TOOLS FOR WRITING

MAKE THE LINK

You will use the past tense in many subjects – for obvious reasons. Since **History** deals with the past, history books need to be in the past tense. The same is true of any subject which looks at events that took place in the past – **Geography** and **Modern Studies** are good examples.

DID YOU KNOW?

Most short stories are told in the past tense. If, however, a story is told in flashback – where the narrator goes back in time to explain past events – then usually such a story will begin in the present tense.

15

OUR EVERYDAY LIVES:

Sometimes we want to talk about an action that took place in the past but is still continuing. To do that we have to use the 'have' form. For example: what is the difference between 'I stayed in Aberdeen for years' and 'I have stayed in Aberdeen for years'? The second sentence lets the reader know that I am still staying in Aberdeen, yet both are past tenses.

TENSES: FUTURE TENSE

We form the future tense in English by using what we call **auxiliary verbs** – the verbs **shall** and **will**.

There are two ways we use the future tense in English:

- I shall walk – the indefinite future tense,

- I shall be walking – which is the future continuous tense.

In informal English and in spoken English, we shorten or contract these verbs – for example, we say 'I'll walk' or 'I'll be walking'.

We normally recognise a verb by its infinitive – 'to go', 'to run', 'to write', 'to photograph'. We can even invent new verbs – 'to goal', 'to be BlackBerried'.

But some verbs – auxiliary verbs, verbs that help main verbs – don't have infinitives. We can't say 'to shall', or 'to might'. Nor have these verbs got past tenses – we can't say 'shalled' or 'mighted' or even 'shalling' or 'mighting'.

TOP TIP

In English, we can also use the present tense of the verb 'to go' to indicate the future. For example, we can say 'I shall go to the cinema tomorrow' or we can say 'I am going to the cinema tomorrow'.

16

BE ACTIVE

TASK 1

Try changing all the verbs in the following television programme review (by *The Herald's* David Belcher, reviewing BBC 1's *Nature's Great Events*) into the future tense to make it seem that the programme is yet to take place.

You might have to change some of it to make sense. The first two verbs have been underlined for you:

JARRINGLY, there <u>was</u> an outbreak of demotic yoof-speak in the closing 10 minutes of Nature's Great Events, a new series which <u>has</u> set itself the task of outlining the most spectacular seasonal wildlife transformations ever wrought by the combined effects of the sun and Mother Earth's rotation.

And so it came to pass that the programme's final segment concentrated on the film-makers of the Beeb's Natural History Unit as they went about capturing the opening show's picture-postcard snowscape, one that was overwhelmingly white, of course, but from time to time red in tooth and claw.

MAKE THE LINK

English can only form the future by using an auxiliary verb – shall or will. Other languages tend to form the future by changing the ending of the verb, i.e. by using inflection. For example, 'I shall swim' translates into **French** as 'Je nagerai' – the 'ai' ending telling us that it is in the first person singular and future tense.

DID YOU KNOW?

Also there are idiomatic uses of the verb 'used to', which vary from one part of the country to another. For example, would you say 'He's been sat there all day' or 'He's been sitting there all day'? Would you say 'My hair needs cut' or 'My hair needs cutting'?

Some of these idioms are Scottish and some are English (i.e. from England) which means that there are geographical differences in the way we use expressions.

OUR EVERYDAY LIVES:

Sometimes we can use verb phrases in an **idiomatic** way – a way that is grammatically natural to native speakers of English.

For example, we can say 'she is going to be able to do her homework' which isn't so much a future tense as a statement about the present. On the other hand 'she is going to play hockey' is future tense.

ADJECTIVES

Learning objectives: an adjective is a word which is used to describe or modify a noun. There are various types of adjectives.

1. Adjectives that are placed before a noun.

2. Adjectives that stand on their own.

3. Adjectives that are used to make comparisons.

TOP TIP

A colour adjective has to be placed as near as possible to the noun it is describing, e.g. that's a beautiful, large, **white** car. A number adjective should go as far away as possible from the noun it is describing, e.g. there were **ten**, large, empty, green bottles on the doorstep.

EXAMPLE

Examples of adjectives that are placed before a noun.

Adjective	What does it do?	Examples
Colour	Describes the colour of something.	Purple hood, pink top, black coat, red face, blue jeans.
Number	Number adjectives are numerals and anything at all to do with numbers.	One, two, three, four… First, second, third… Single, double, treble… Both, many, few.

Examples of adjectives that stand on their own:

*   Your dinner is **ready**.

*   My hair is **dry**.

*   The cinema is **busy**.

Examples of adjectives that are used to make comparisons:

*   Drew is **smaller** than Harry.

*   Fiona is **kinder** than Kylie.

*   Eilidh is **more intelligent** than Shaun.

*   Your school bag is **less heavy** than mine.

18

BE ACTIVE

TASK 1

The following are lists of nouns along with some adjectives. Arrange the adjectives into the correct order to describe the noun.

1. bottles: wide-necked, green, large, ten

2. shelves: book-lined, wooden, four, pine-coloured, broad

3. ships: cruise, two, luxury, six-berth, white

4. daffodils; golden, tall, twelve

5. wasps; angry, striped, forty, stinging, yellow-black

TASK 2

Newspapers are very fond of adjectives. With the permission of the person who bought the newspaper, cut out headlines where an adjective has been used.

TASK 3

Try writing your own advertising copy. You are designing an advert to attract people to your school. Think carefully of the adjectives you would choose.

TASK 4

Adjectives are also used by advertisers. Again, collect as many adjectives as you can from adverts (newspapers, magazines, television, radio) and discuss in your groups what each adjective actually does for the product advertised. Are there any claims that cannot be justified?

TASK 5

Now make a list of as many Scots adjectives as you can. Read To a Mouse by Robert Burns. He uses the adjectives 'wee', 'sleekit', 'cow'rin', and 'tim'rous' to describe the mouse. Think of some Scots adjectives to describe a hamburger from your favourite fast-food outlet.

TOOLS FOR WRITING

MAKE THE LINK

Find out from the **Modern Languages** department where the colour and the number adjectives go in the language that you are studying. Is the rule different from English?

DID YOU KNOW?

Some writers feel that they make their writing more powerful if they include many adjectives, but you can also make your writing more powerful by using strong verbs. Look, for example, at the following sentence from George Orwell's *Marrakech*. He is describing the life of the average labourer in Marrakech in the 1930s.

> They rise out of the earth, they sweat and starve for a few years, and they sink back into the nameless mounds of the graveyard and nobody notices that they are gone.

It's the verbs in that sentence that make it so striking – there are very few adjectives.

19

OUR EVERYDAY LIVES:

Adjectives come in four basic forms that we use every day.

1. Before a noun – 'The tall ship'.

2. After the verb 'to be' – 'That ship is tall'.

3. After an intensifier – 'That ship is really tall' or 'That ship is very tall.

4. When we make a comparison – 'That ship is taller than that other ship' or 'That ship is the tallest'.

PUNCTUATION

Learning objectives: to learn how to recognise and use basic punctuation marks.

Being able to punctuate properly is an important tool for helping the reader to make sense of a piece of written text.

The writer has to know the function of the various punctuation marks available to him or her in order to convey meaning.

The reader has to have enough knowledge of these same marks in order to understand them properly, so that the writer's meaning can be grasped.

TOP TIP

Here is an easy way of remembering how to use the apostrophe: put the apostrophe before the 's' unless the plural already ends in an 's', in which case just add the apostrophe, e.g. the dog's dish; the dogs' dishes.

20

.	Full stop – the main function of the full stop is to signal the end of a sentence.
?	The question mark – indicates that a question is being asked.
!	The exclamation mark – the exclamation mark can establish surprise or help convey deep emotion. It can also suggest that the remark being made should be taken humorously.
,	Comma – the comma is mainly used to clarify meaning, e.g. remove the commas from the following sentence and you will see how the meaning is altered – 'The number is being played live, in response to many requests, by Take That.' It can also be used to separate words or items in lists (e.g. the zoo has elephants, tigers, penguins, eagles and a polar bear), and before and after someone's name, e.g. 'hello, Heidi, how are you today?'
" "	Inverted Commas – inverted commas are sometimes also called speech marks or quotation marks and can appear as double marks ("…") or as single marks ('…'). They are usually used to show words actually spoken, and also quoted words.
'	Apostrophe – all that the apostrophe means is that there is a letter missing from a word that has been shortened (abbreviated). For example, 'can't' is the abbreviated form of 'cannot', 'don't' is the abbreviated form of 'do not'. The apostrophe can also indicate possession, e.g. 'the girl's bag' – meaning 'the bag belonging to the girl', 'the boy's iPod' meaning 'the iPod belonging to the boy'.

BE ACTIVE

The easiest way to understand the importance of punctuation is to remove it from a piece of writing and then try to make sense of the text.

TASK 1

Here is an extract from *The Moon is Down* by John Steinbeck. Write out the paragraph inserting punctuation.

> beside the fireplace old doctor winter sat bearded and simple and benign historian and physician to the town he watched in amazement while his thumbs rolled over and over on his lap doctor winter was a man so simple that only a profound man would know him as profound he looked up at joseph the mayor's serving man to see whether joseph had observed the rolling wonders of his thumbs eleven oclock doctor winter asked and joseph answered abstractedly yes sir the note said eleven you read the note no sir his excellency read the note to me and joseph went about testing each of the gilded chairs to see whether it had moved since he had last placed it

TASK 2

Rewrite the following sentences more formally, so that you don't (do not) need the apostrophe.

- That boy can't ski.
- The teacher's desk isn't as tidy as usual.
- I would've gone if you'd've come with me.
- 'Ah've 'eard it all now, ev'ry 'scuse goin'.

TASK 3

The sign right indicates the direction of the offices belonging to – well, can we tell? Do the offices belong to one minister or more than one minister? Why can't we tell?

Ministers Offices
Oifis nam Ministearan

MAKE THE LINK

As you know, in English we use the apostrophe to indicate that a letter s is missing. Find out whether other European languages can use the apostrophe in a similar way – that is to indicate abbreviated words and to indicate possession. How, for example, do you translate the following sentences into French, Spanish or German?

- The boy said he wasn't able to do his friend's homework.
- His dog isn't as clever as his sister's.
- Because it's so hot today, I'm going swimming.
- What's your brother's favourite food?
- My lizard's called Vlad and he's fond of blueberries.

DID YOU KNOW?

The way we punctuate sentences changes over time. Modern punctuation is quite different from the way writers used punctuation in the 19th century, for example. You need to know how to use today's punctuation marks correctly and how to recognise what they signal in a piece of prose.

OUR EVERYDAY LIVES:

A common mistake nowadays is what we call 'the comma splice' where an unskilful writer tries to join or 'splice' two units of sense together using only a comma. The important thing to know is that commas cannot join items. If your teacher points out a comma splice in your writing you can fix it by replacing the comma with a conjunction – an 'and', for example.

SPELLING

Unlike other languages, English spelling is not closely related to the way we pronounce words. Of course, spelling has to attempt to represent the way we pronounce words but look at the exceptions.

For example, take the following words – bough, cough, tough, plough, though, through, lough (Irish for 'loch'). All are pronounced quite differently, yet all are spelt in the same way.

Take words such as 'science' and 'conscience' and 'omniscience' – again all pronounced differently. Then there's 'blood' and 'mud', spelt differently but with the same vowel sound.

EXAMPLE

There are no spelling rules as such, but there are guidelines to help you. But remember to learn the exceptions to the guidelines.

1. With words which have prefixes and/or suffixes, add the prefix and/or suffix to the stock word and this will help your spelling.

dis	+ appear	=	disappear
dis	+ solve	=	dissolve
im	+ moral	=	immoral
un	+ necessary	=	unnecessary
in	+ valuable	=	invaluable
in	+ numerate	=	innumerate

2. For this guideline you need to know the difference between short and long vowel sounds. A short vowel is pronounced as in hat, fed, pin, slop, and cut and long vowel sounds are as in hate, feed, pine, slope and cute.

    The guideline is fairly complex but useful. In words ending in –ing, where the vowel before the –ing is short, then the consonant is doubled. The rule isn't 100% foolproof, but it is a good guide.

begin	+ n + ing	=	beginning
spin	+ n + ing	=	spinning
refer	+ r + ing	=	referring
twin	+ n + ing	=	twinning
pine (drop the e)	+ ing	=	pining
line (drop the e)	+ ing	=	lining
sneak	+ ing	=	sneaking
dine (drop the e)	+ ing	=	dining room

3. In a two syllable word, however, where the second syllable is weak (that is, where the syllable is unstressed), you do not double the consonant before adding –ing. For example:

    In the word snigger, the –er is weak, the stress comes on the first syllable (we say snigger), therefore keep the r single.

    In the word benefit, the –fit is weak, therefore the t remains single.

    Similarly, in the word target the –et is weak, therefore the t remains single.

4. And then there is the old rule: i before e except after c, with certain exceptions, such as seize.

TOP TIP
Pay attention to the context. 'b4' may be acceptable in the context of emails and text messages but in the context of a formal essay it is unsuitable.

22

BE ACTIVE

There is only one way to improve your spelling – you have to learn how to spell certain words – it won't come to you naturally. You just have to remember that necessary has one 'c' and a double 's' and that embarrass has a double 'r' and a double 's'. The word harass on the other hand has only one 'r' and a double 's'.

You need to be able to spell the following words accurately:

a lot (two separate words)	does	principal (main or chief)
	doesn't	
	excite	principle (standards / beliefs)
across	explained	
advice (noun)	fascinated	
to advise (verb)	fierce	probably
	giraffe	queue
all right (two separate words)	guard	rich
	habit	seize
	heard	separate
annoyed	humble	servant
anxious	imagine	several
apology	imagination	shepherd
apartment	in fact (two separate words)	snapped
apologies		souvenir
attention		straight
because	interest	suicide
beginning	jealous	tomorrow
behaviour	jealousy	treasure
bought	lightning	threatens
brochures	minutes	tried
colleague	mentions	try / tries
colour	occasionally	until
concentrate	opportunity	weather
conjure	peril	weird
criticise	practice (noun)	were
definitely	to practise (verb)	where
desert		whether
disappeared	precisely	wonderful

TOOLS FOR WRITING

MAKE THE LINK

Mandarin has about 50 000 characters. In the 1960s, around 2000 of these were simplified and are now known as 'simplified characters'. The other characters are known as 'traditional' or 'complex' characters. To read and write Mandarin you need to know about 2000 characters!

DID YOU KNOW?

In recent times, written language has begun to change the spoken language – it has always been the other way round. Perhaps the change began with television, Eastenders in particular, where the use of spoken cockney (the language spoken by some Londoners) began to move northwards, so that people in the central belt of Scotland began to use the 'f' sound instead of 'th', as in 'yoofs' for 'youths', 'free' for 'three', 'teef' for 'teeth', 'anyfink' for 'anything', 'choose dye' for 'Tuesday'. That trend has been increasingly developed by the widespread use of email and phone texts.

Scotland has had for centuries its own languages and its own regional accents. But because of email, chat rooms, and texts, there is a spread of what is called Estuary English – the accent and vocabulary used by people living in the areas around the estuary of the River Thames. That accent is now being used in the written mode – words such as 'wiv' for 'with', 'wanna' for 'want to', 'yer' for 'yes' are all being accepted as words in the written mode.

OUR EVERYDAY LIVES:

Tabloid newspapers often spell according to sound (sometimes referred to as spelling phonetically). For example, when the Royal Navy sank the General Belgrano, an enemy battleship, during the Falklands War, *The Sun* newspaper ran the massive headline 'Gotcha'.

WHY DO WE WRITE?

Throughout secondary school, you will be asked to do a lot of writing in your English classes. There are all kinds of reasons why we write:

- note taking,
- writing out instructions for someone to follow,
- writing to express our views on a topic,
- making a list,
- leaving a note for your mum / dad / brother / sister / friend,
- sending a text,
- sending an email,
- report writing,
- writing a story,
- writing a poem,
- writing about an experience.

Although these may be the main reasons for writing, you can probably think of even more!

All types of text have a few things in common.

- First of all, each type of writing has to have a **purpose**, a reason for committing pen to paper (or fingers to keyboard).
- Secondly, each piece of writing has to have the right kind of **structure** (the way that it is put together).
- Thirdly, writing has to have a **reader**, even if the reader is only yourself. But if someone is going to read your text, then it has to be written with that person in mind.
- Fourthly, text has to be written in an appropriate language: we use the term **register** to describe the words and phrases that are appropriate for the reader (or listener, if we are dealing with talking skills).

When we write we have to remember each of these **four aspects of writing**:

- **purpose**,
- **structure**,
- **reader**,
- **register**.

The purpose of your writing will help you to decide the structure and the reader will help you to decide on the register.

EXAMPLE

You text your friend to find out where he is.

You type in: 'wer r u?'

Purpose – to find out where your friend is.

Structure – the fact that you are using a mobile phone will help determine the structure. You use a short phrase, in the form of a question, typed directly into your phone.

Reader – as your friend, knows the register of mobile phone language, the language is appropriate.

Register – the spelling, the abbreviations, the use of the single consonant to form one sound and the use of a vowel for a word are all appropriate for text language, especially to a friend, who will have knowledge of the language and be able to decode it.

TOP TIP

It's the purpose of your writing that gives it structure. For example, you are on holiday and want to send your friend a postcard to let him or her know how much you are enjoying it. What do you do? Obviously you buy the postcard and then the fact that you want to tell your friend about your enjoyment determines what you say.

24

BE ACTIVE

TASK 1

Write out what you would want to say on a postcard. Maybe you want to make your friend jealous of the good time you are having – an added purpose! Make sure that you structure what you say so as to convey that idea.

TASK 2

Now try writing a fiction paragraph. The purpose is to create a scene set on a tropical island, like paradise, upon which three boys have been shipwrecked. Make the structure of your sentences long and flowing to capture the idea of the slow sweep of the wind on the palm trees and sand.

Keep in mind your reader and make sure that your register is appropriate to the setting.

TASK 3

Now write a paragraph set on the same island but this time there's a tropical storm lashing it.

MAKE THE LINK

Writing and reading are just like two sides of the same coin. In other words, as you develop your reading skills you begin to adopt these same skills in your own writing, and as you develop those skills in your writing you become more and more aware of reading skills.

You almost 'paint' pictures with words, much as you paint scenes in your **art** class.

DID YOU KNOW?

There are over a million words in the English language. One way to build up your vocabulary is to buy a small A5 notebook and write down in it all the unfamiliar words that you come across everyday.

You can also use your notebook to remind you of words that you can use in you writing.

OUR EVERYDAY LIVES:

You will be astonished by the amount you write in any given day. But whether it's simple notes, a text, an email, a conversation in a chat room, or a formal essay, you should take pride in what you write and make sure, above all, that it's legible. Even a shopping list requires a structure.

MORE ABOUT REGISTER

Learning objective: register is important when writing a text because it helps you to communicate well with others in a way that suits your purpose and your audience.

The example below shows how we use register when speaking to different people.

TOP TIP
So far, we have worked out that any piece of writing has to consider four aspects: purpose, structure, reader, register. All four of these aspects are of equal importance, so whenever you write pay close attention to all of them.

EXAMPLE

At school one lunchtime, a food-fight takes place in the canteen when there are no teachers present. You see everything. Your best friend missed it and you can't wait to tell him what happened and how the head boy got covered in custard. But when the rector finds out that you were the main witness, he calls you to his office to hear your version. After you have told the rector what you saw, he asks to repeat the story to several other teachers. Then, at home that evening, you tell your parents about the food fight.

In total, you have told the story to:

* your friend
* the rector
* the entire senior management team of the school
* your parents.

In this example, you have to tell the story of the food fight to four different audiences.

Now think about it – do you tell the events in exactly the same way to all four groups of people, or do you change your story to suit your audience? Would you use exactly the same words (vocabulary), sentence structure, style, tone with all four groups?

Or would you alter the vocabulary, sentence structure, style, and tone that are appropriate for your friends when you retell the story to the rector?

In other words, register has to do with the appropriateness of language in different situations.

* CREATING TEXTS *

BE ACTIVE

TASK 1

Look again at the example on the previous page. Write out the story as you would tell it to the rector.

TASK 2

Here is a piece taken from the *Sunday Herald's* television pages. The critic makes a comment about the Saturday night programme *Demons*. He takes the opportunity to comment on the entire television output for the evening.

> **Demons**
> **7.40pm, ITV**
> So. The other day on the radio I heard this story, about how British Saturday night TV was better now than it ever has been. Like, ever, right? Uh-huh. Well. Man. I'll tell you. Maybe it's just me. But I'm not feeling that. I mean, there have been some bad Saturday nights of TV before now, right? But this – Saturday, January 17, 2009? That date will live in infamy as the worst Saturday night's TV ever. I mean, it's really, really bad. The best thing on TV tonight is Demons – and Demons is one of the worst programmes ever made.

Working in pairs, discuss how this text has been written, paying attention to register. Then, still working in pairs, rewrite this article, altering the register to make the piece much more formal and not at all humorous.

TASK 3

When your mum tells you that you can invite your friend for a meal on Saturday night, you decide to send him/her an email in which you set out the invitation and instructions about how to get to your house. Write the email.

TASK 4

At home, or in your Home Economics class, write out the recipe of the meal you are going to cook, copying a true style of a typical recipe.

MAKE THE LINK

Writing is not a skill used only in the English classroom. All your teachers will ask you at some time or other to write – maybe you have to write up a science experiment in **Physics** or take notes in **Geography**. Whatever you are asked to write remember to pay attention to purpose, structure, reader (even if the reader is yourself at a later date), and register.

Maybe you have to use presentation software as part of **Information and Communication Technology** (ICT). That means that we have to be able to set out points on a screen – points that are not only clear and concise, but also with attention having been paid to their layout and design.

DID YOU KNOW?

Planning is a very important part of writing. A plan can be anything from an outline of the paragraphs, to a mindmap, to a spider diagram. The advantage of a plan is that you don't lose sight of your purpose. It's so easy to begin an essay and wander off, losing track of what it was you were going to write about, but with a plan that won't happen. A plan also means that you remember all your points!

OUR EVERYDAY LIVES:

Sometimes we write just for the fun of it – because we like rhyme or because we want to remember our everyday experiences by writing about them.

Maybe you keep a diary – partly to record events but also, perhaps, to capture your emotions and feelings, where you spend some time trying to articulate (put into words) everyday experiences in ways that are rewarding and personal.

ESSAY WRITING

Learning objective: to understand what is meant by 'an essay', what the requirements of essay writing are, and to have a clear idea of how to go about writing one.

Introducing essays

In your time in the English Department, you'll learn how to write different kinds of essays.

- Essays about a personal experience.
- Essays which parody (make fun of) another literary form.
- Essays which are imaginative or creative, such as a short story or a poem.

- Essays which give information.
- Essays which state ideas and/or which set out arguments and/or which weigh up a topic.

You will also be asked to write essays which talk about a piece of literature that you have studied in class.

In this book, we will examine how to write the first two of these – essays which set out a personal experience and essays which parody another story.

EXAMPLE

Let's begin with the personal essay. What is required? You may already have tried writing personal essays at Primary school. It's where you write about a personal experience – something that has happened to you personally. It could be a story about some event that took place on your holiday or it could be about a situation where you were, perhaps, let down by a friend. The point is that it has to be about something you have experienced, something particular that has happened to you.

But a personal essay shouldn't just be about a series of events – you should try to get across some idea of the kind of person you are and/or you should try to reflect on your experience – how did it make you feel? Sad? Happy? Thoughtful? Did you learn anything from it?

The great thing about personal essays is that you get a chance to write about yourself – and there is no subject about which you know more!

Always bear in mind who you are writing for and make sure that you entertain that person, making him or her want to read on. You will be marked according to how well you can express your personal feelings or emotional reactions.

TOP TIP

In a personal essay, what matters is not just writing about what you did, but also about how you felt or what you learned from the experience (whatever that was).

28

BE ACTIVE

QUICK TASK

Now it's your turn to write an essay. The subject is: a time when you felt badly let down.

Think of a time when someone – your mum, dad, sister, brother, best friend – promised something but didn't deliver. Or when someone insulted you or made some unsympathetic comment about you or a member of your family. Or maybe you weren't let down by a person, as such; maybe you were let down because something to which you were looking forward to was cancelled – for example, a party or a holiday.

Once you have thought of a suitable occasion when you felt let down, you can start your plan – and that is the subject of the next section.

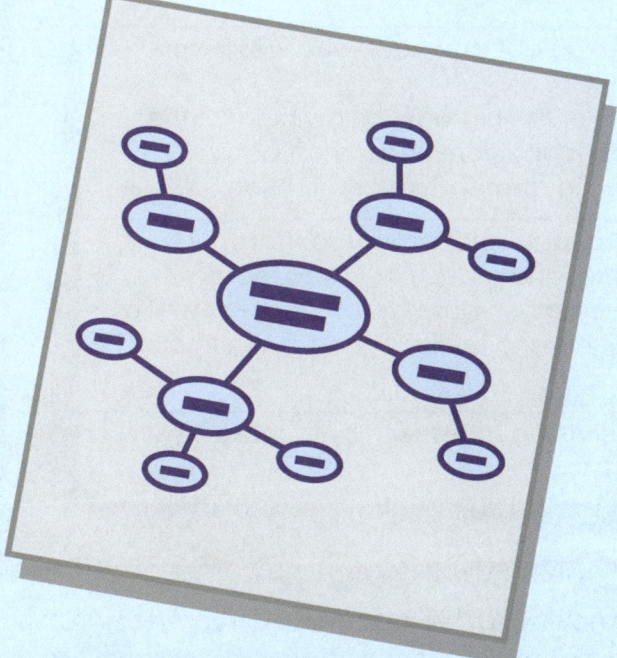

Try to remember what we said about adjectives and verbs! It is more important to use really strong, striking verbs than it is to pepper your essay with adjectives.

MAKE THE LINK

There is a link between writing and reading. As you develop new reading skills you also learn to start using those skills in your writing. As you learn how to recognise and analyse, say, a writer's use of metaphor, so you can start using metaphor in the same kind of way.

Usually the only departments that will ask you to write a personal essay are **English** and **Modern Languages**. But other departments will still want you to write essays. Find out what other departments, such as **History**, expect of you when you are asked to write essays for them.

DID YOU KNOW?

Do you keep a diary? What else is a diary but an attempt to come to terms with what's happening around you? We can all keep diaries that list events – 'Monday 30 August – went to cinema and saw the latest Bond film' – but sometimes we record more personal things, such as how we are feeling, what our relationships are with other people, or any problems that we are having. The personal essay is quite like those kind of diary entries, though not in the same style.

29

OUR EVERYDAY LIVES:

Actually it's what happens in our everyday lives that make the best subjects for the personal essay. It doesn't have to be anything dramatic or earth-shattering – just an ordinary, everyday event which you write about in an interesting way. It's the quality of the writing itself that captures the reader's attention.

STRUCTURE: MAKING AN ESSAY PLAN

Learning objective: how to write a plan for your essay.

The best way to decide a suitable structure for an essay is to plan the essay. Essay plans do not have to be huge: you can keep it very simple. The main points to plan are:

- **introduction**,
- **main body of the essay**,
- **reflection**, though this should run through the essay
- **conclusion**.

TOP TIP

Make an essay plan for every essay you write from now on, all the way through school. It will make writing essays much easier!

EXAMPLE

Let's try working out a plan for this essay: My first day at secondary school:

Introduction	You remember your first day at secondary school. Some detailed description of when/where/weather (weather is useful to include as it can help establish mood – we associate rain with sadness and sunshine with laughter and fun).
Main body of the essay	Describe what happened, e.g. how you got to school, who was in your class, which new subjects you started. Try to capture the build-up to whatever the highlight or low point of the day was: climax is an important part of any story and is most powerful if you give it a slow build-up. Try to create atmosphere and tension.
Reflection (for personal experience essays)	Include (where appropriate) your thoughts and feelings so that your reader knows how you felt at the time, and maybe how you feel now. Try to communicate your emotions – feeling nervous, shy, excited – as well as your thoughts on the situation. Thoughts and feelings need to run through a personal experience essay.
Conclusion	The conclusion is where you pull everything together – try to make it as interesting as you can.

Remember also your **reader**: decide who that person is and write to and for him or her. In other words, write your essay to someone specific. That person could be your teacher, but it might not – it could be your mum, your friend, or even your Aunt Matilda.

When you send a postcard from your holiday to someone you know, you deliberately write your message with that person in mind – you know what will appeal to him or her, which is what makes your postcard interesting. It should be the same with your essay. Write it for someone.

And finally, you have to choose an appropriate **register**. As you now know, register is the appropriate use of vocabulary, sentence structure, and tone in your writing.

30

* CREATING TEXTS *

BE ACTIVE

Try not to think of essay writing as a hoop to be jumped through. Take your time and think about the essay.

Sometimes it helps to discuss the experience that you want to write about – with your teacher, with your partner in the classroom, or with your group. Then think carefully about how you write it – try to avoid too many adjectives, but use strong, active verbs to give your writing energy.

TASK 1

In a group, plan a personal essay about the most disastrous holiday in your life so far, drawing on each other's experience as much as possible.

TASK 2

Now working in pairs, plan an essay that is going to deal with the most important piece of technology in your lives.

First of all agree what the piece of technology is then go on and plan an essay where you set out why you cannot live without it.

MAKE THE LINK

All essay writing should be planned which means that any essay given to you by another department – **History**, **Geography**, **Modern Languages** – should be planned too. Ask your subject teachers about ways in which you can plan the essays that they ask you to write. In other subjects, you may learn about mind maps, linear notes, diagrams and other methods of planning writing.

DID YOU KNOW?

Tone just means the mood of writing: does the writer feel anger or bitterness or sarcasm or nostalgia or celebration or humour? Look at how writers use words to set a particular tone, and experiment with using tone yourself in your own writing.

OUR EVERYDAY LIVES:

A plan, especially for a short piece of work, can of course be all in your head. For example, ask your parents about their shopping lists. Is it entirely random? Shoes written down beside sausages, CDs written after ice cream, jeans next to apples? Or do they compile it shop by shop – all the clothes items on one list, all the groceries on another? Even if their entire shopping is within the supermarket, is the list random or do they group the items according to types: all the cleaning materials on one part of the list, all the household goods on another, the frozen foods on another, and so on? Just as your mum or dad organises – plans – the shopping list, so you have to organise – plan – your essay writing.

EXAMPLE: PARODIES

Learning objective: how to parody the style of an existing story and to ensure an understanding of what is meant by 'subversion'.

Essays which parody another story can be great fun. An example will make things clearer. You all know the story of Goldilocks and the Three Bears – now read Roald Dahl's version below.

Goldilocks and the Three Bears

Goldilocks and the Three Bears
This famous wicked little tale
Should never have been put on sale.
It is a mystery to me
Why loving parents cannot see
That this is actually a book
About a brazen little crook.
Had I the chance I wouldn't fail
To clap young Goldilocks in jail.
Now just imagine how you'd feel
If you had cooked a lovely meal,
Delicious porridge, steaming hot,
Fresh coffee in the coffee-pot,
With maybe toast and marmalade,
The table beautifully laid,
One place for you and one for dad,
Another for your little lad.
Then dad cries, 'Golly-gosh! Gee-whizz!
Oh cripes! How hot this porridge is!
Let's take a walk along the street
Until it's cold enough to eat.'
He adds 'An early morning stroll
Is good for people on the whole
It makes your appetite improve
It also helps your bowels to move.'
No proper wife would dare to question
Such a sensible suggestion,
Above all not at breakfast-time
When men are seldom at their prime.
No sooner are you down the road
Than Goldilocks that little toad
That nosey thieving little louse,
Comes sneaking in your empty house.
She looks around. She quickly notes.
Three bowl's brimful of porridge oats.
And while still standing on her feet,
She grabs a spoon and starts to eat.
I say again, how would you feel
If you had made this lovely meal

And some delinquent little tot
Broke in and gobbled up the lot?
But wait! That's not the worst of it!
Now comes the most distressing bit.
You are of course a house-proud wife,
And all your happy married life
You have collected lovely things
Like gilded cherubs wearing wings,
And furniture by Chippendale
Bought at some famous auction sale.
But your most special valued treasure,
The piece that gives you endless pleasure,
Is one small children's dining chair,
Elizabethan, very rare.
It is in fact your joy and pride
Passed down to you on grandma's side.
But Goldilocks like many freaks,
Does not appreciate antiques.
She doesn't care, she doesn't mind,
And now she plonks her fat behind
Upon this dainty precious chair,
And crunch! It busts beyond repair.
A nice girl would at once exclaim,
'Oh dear! Oh heavens! What a shame!'
Not Goldie. She begins to swear.
She bellows, 'What a lousy chair!'
And uses one disgusting word
That luckily you've never heard.
(I dare not write it, even hint it.
Nobody would ever print it.)
You'd think by now this little skunk
Would have the sense to do a bunk.
But no, I very much regret
She hasn't nearly finished yet.
Deciding she would like a rest,
She says, 'Let's see which bed is best.'
Upstairs she goes and tries all three.
(Here comes the next catastrophe.)
Most educated people choose
To rid themselves of socks and shoes
Before they clamber into bed.
But Goldie didn't give a shred.

Her filthy shoes were thick with grime,
And mud and mush and slush and slime.
Worse still, upon the heel of one
Was something that a dog had done.
I say once more, what would you think
If all this horrid dirt and stink
Was smeared upon your eiderdown
By this revolting little clown?
(The famous story has no clues
To show the girl removed her shoes.)
Oh, what a tale of crime on crime!
Let's check it for a second time.

Crime One, the prosecution's case:
She breaks and enters someone's place.

Crime Two: the prosecutor notes:
She steals a bowl of porridge oats.

Crime Three: She breaks a precious chair
Belonging to the Baby Bear.

Crime Four: She smears each spotless sheet
With filthy messes from her feet.

A judge would say without a blink,
'Ten years hard labour in the clink!'
But in the book, as you will see,
The little beast gets off scot-free,
While tiny children near and far
Shout: 'Goody-good! Hooray! Hurrah!'
'Poor darling Goldilocks!' they say,
'Thank goodness that she got away!'
Myself, I think I'd rather send
Young Goldie to a sticky end.
'Oh daddy!' cried the Baby Bear,
'My porridge gone! It isn't fair!'
'Then go upstairs,' the Big Bear said,
'Your porridge is upon the bed.
'But as it's inside mademoiselle,
'You'll have to eat her up as well.'

Roald Dahl has obviously quite considerably changed the story of Goldilocks and the Three Bears. He has, to use the technical terminology, subverted the story of Goldilocks to make Goldilocks out to be a baddie.

32

✱ CREATING TEXTS ✱

BE ACTIVE

QUICK TASK

For this essay, work in pairs. Together, decide which fairy tale or well-known story you are going to subvert. But again please bear the four aspects of writing in mind:

- **purpose**,
- **structure**,
- **reader**,
- **register**.

The **purpose** is to subvert a well-know story or fairy tale so that you stand its moral on its head. Or, in another sense, you subvert the story by modernising it, giving it a 21st-century twist. For example, you could rewrite *Little Red Riding Hood* so that the little girl gets the better of the wolf – pulls her handgun from her Louis Vuitton handbag and shoots him dead. Or Cinderella could be an intelligent, scheming, resourceful young woman and Prince Charming an ineffectual wimp, whom she uses just to get her revenge on her sisters.

The **structure** is up to the pair of you: as with Roald Dahl's retelling of the Goldilocks story, you could structure your essay as a poem.

Remember what has already been said about the intended **reader** of your story – are you writing for a child, a young adult or an adult? And the **register** would have to use the vocabulary, sentence structure ('Once upon a time...'), and tone of a fairy story.

TOP TIP

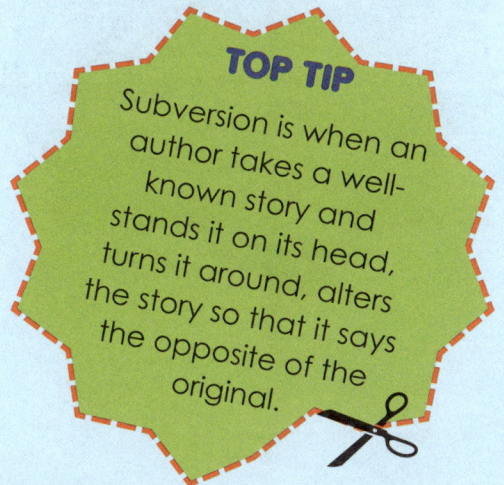

Subversion is when an author takes a well-known story and stands it on its head, turns it around, alters the story so that it says the opposite of the original.

CREATING TEXTS

MAKE THE LINK

Subversion is not only an important aspect of essay writing – or even of novel writing – but it is also used in films, television programmes and even in advertising. Try to think of any television or magazine advertisements that use subversion – where they take a story and change it round to make a clever or amusing point.

You also study newspaper articles and advertising in **Modern Studies** and **Business Studies** – but not always for the same reasons!

DID YOU KNOW?

Roald Dahl wrote many stories for children (and also for adults). His autobiography about his childhood – called *Boy: Tales of Childhood* makes fascinating reading and shows how many things that happened to him as a child were inspirational afterwards in providing ideas for his stories.

33

OUR EVERYDAY LIVES:

Sometimes the stories we watch as television programmes or as films in the cinema are based on well-known fairy tales. The ideas behind the *Cinderella* story (rags-to-riches, cruel step-parents, nasty brothers or sisters), for example, form the basis of many stories as does the tale of *David and Goliath* (the success of the little man against huge odds).

INTRODUCTION TO READING SKILLS

Learning objective: to improve your reading abilities.

Throughout your English course, from First Year right through to the Higher English course, your reading skills are tested in two ways.

Study of Literary Texts

You will be given all kinds of literary texts to read: novels, non-fiction texts, drama and poetry. To read these effectively and with enjoyment, you have to develop skills in analysis and evaluation. These skills are tested by getting you to write **critical essays** where you explore aspects of the texts – these will be discussed in the next chapter.

Close Reading

Your reading skills are also tested by **close reading** where you are given a passage to read, followed by questions that will test your understanding of what you have just read. You may also be asked some questions that ask you to analyse how certain written effects have been achieved, and occasionally you might be asked to evaluate these effects.

You will have to develop reading skills that will enable you to:

* identify the purpose of a text,
* find and use information that you have found in a text,
* make inferences from a text, i.e. be able to deduce information from a text,
* make comparisons between texts,
* recognise a text that is trying to persuade you to a particular point of view.

TOP TIP
Remember the four aspects of writing – **purpose, structure, reader** and **register**. You can apply these to reading as well. For example, what is the purpose of a text? Which kind of reader is it aimed at?

34

UNDERSTANDING ★

BE ACTIVE

TASK 1

Think about what you enjoy reading – do you like novels, or magazines, or Manga?

Have you read anything in class that you particularly liked? Make a list of three or four texts that you've enjoyed reading.

Then add a short sentence making clear to a classmate why you liked each text.

TASK 2

Now, in pairs, compare lists and try to explain to each other why you liked these texts more than others.

TASK 3

Can you think of examples of texts that you read every day for information? Examples might include bus timetables, TV guides and internet sites.

Again in pairs, make a list of ten types of texts that you read for information.

Now, in pairs, compare lists and expand on your reasons for liking these texts. Make sure you listen as well as talk.

READING FOR UNDERSTANDING

MAKE THE LINK

Reading is an important skill for every subject! In **Home Economics** we learn the importance of reading recipes correctly. In **History**, we learn the importance of analysing information from different types of text. In **Modern Studies**, we learn about texts such as newspapers which may try to influence our opinion. And in every subject, when we have to answer written questions, we are taught the importance of reading the questions accurately!

DID YOU KNOW?

Some people make a career out of reading. For example, some fiction publishers employ readers to read new novels and help decide whether they should be published or not.

35

OUR EVERYDAY LIVES:

If you had to take a note of just how often you read something on any given day, you might be astonished at the amount and variety of material that you read, skim, scan and digest. From newspaper headlines, to adverts on billboards, to video game instructions to class timetables, you read an enormous amount every day.

IDENTIFYING PURPOSE

There is a close link between writing skills and reading skills. They are almost like two sides of the same coin. The four aspects of writing – **purpose**, **structure**, **reader**, **and register** – apply just as much when it comes to reading skills. Every text has to have a purpose, a structure, be written with a reader in mind, and be in a register that is appropriate to the reader.

EXAMPLE

IT'S OFFICIAL: UEFA ADMIT IT AT LAST

WE WOZ ROBBED

Ref's call that KO'd Scotland was wrong

Look at the headline above, from the front page of the *News of the World* [8 Feb 2009]. Ask yourself: what is the **purpose** of the headline? Is it to give information, to catch people's interest, to annoy, to get sympathy? How is it **structured**? Is it a statement or a question? Is it grammatically correct? How should it read if it were to be written formally? What is the purpose of the apostrophe in 'Ref's' and 'KO'd'? Why do you think the headline and the sub-headline have been structured this way (again, think of purpose)? Who is the intended **reader**? A lawyer, a teacher, an artist, a priest, a football fan? What is the **register**? Is it formal, informal, serious, witty, angry, pleading? Give reasons for your answers.

TOP TIP
Remember that everything is a text – from the label on the side of a tin of beans, to a bus timetable, to a Shakespeare play.

36

UNDERSTANDING *

Look at the labels below.

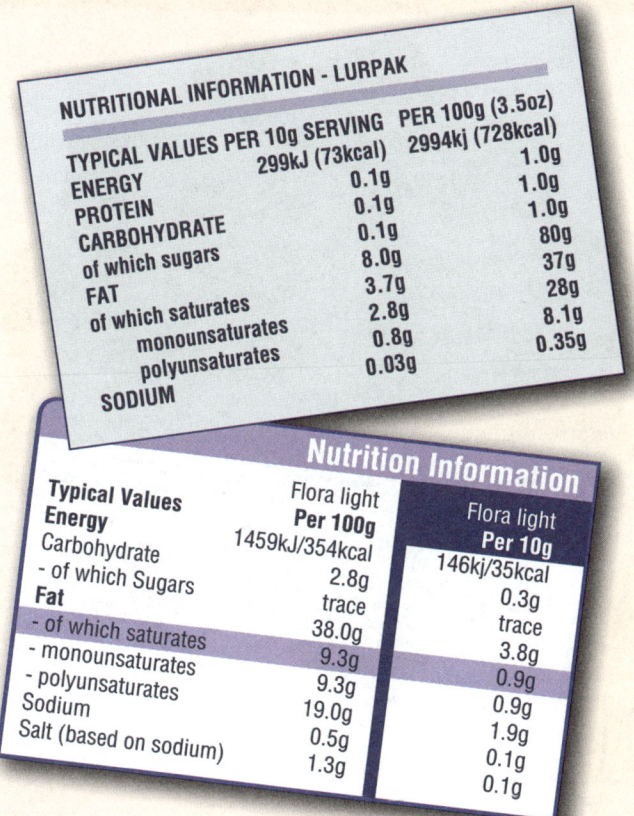

NUTRITIONAL INFORMATION - LURPAK		
TYPICAL VALUES	PER 10g SERVING 299kJ (73kcal)	PER 100g (3.5oz) 2994kj (728kcal)
ENERGY	0.1g	1.0g
PROTEIN	0.1g	1.0g
CARBOHYDRATE	0.1g	1.0g
of which sugars	8.0g	80g
FAT	3.7g	37g
of which saturates	2.8g	28g
monounsaturates	0.8g	8.1g
polyunsaturates	0.03g	0.35g
SODIUM		

Nutrition Information		
Typical Values	Flora light Per 100g	Flora light Per 10g
Energy	1459kJ/354kcal	146kj/35kcal
Carbohydrate		
- of which Sugars	2.8g	0.3g
Fat	trace	trace
- of which saturates	38.0g	3.8g
- monounsaturates	9.3g	0.9g
- polyunsaturates	9.3g	0.9g
Sodium	19.0g	1.9g
Salt (based on sodium)	0.5g	0.1g
	1.3g	0.1g

TASK 1

Try to determine the purpose of these labels. What are the labels for? Who is the intended reader of these texts?

TASK 2

Answer the following questions, based on the information provided by the texts – you will need to make comparisons between the texts.

a) How many calories does each 10g portion contain?
b) Which of the spreads contains more saturated fat?
c) Which spread is salt free?
d) Which spread contains additives?

TASK 3

Working in pairs, compare the texts again. Which do you think is the healthier option and why?

READING FOR UNDERSTANDING

MAKE THE LINK

In **Home Economics**, we learn about food labels and good nutrition. In **Modern Studies**, we study newspapers. In **Maths**, we learn about percentages.

DID YOU KNOW?

Spreads such as Lurpak and Flora Light should be eaten in moderation, as part of a healthy, balanced diet. The Eatwell plate shows us how much of each food type we should eat, to maintain health and well-being.

OUR EVERYDAY LIVES:

Purpose can decide structure, and we can see an example of this every day by looking at road signs. Road signs have three distinct purposes: signs that give warnings, signs that have to be obeyed and signs that inform. Each of these purposes is shown in the very structure of the sign.

Warning signs are triangular.

 Signs that have to be obeyed are circular.

 Signs that give information are rectangular.

The purpose of any given road sign determines its structure and the structure is in the form of the sign shape.

FINDING AND USING INFORMATION FROM TEXTS

Sometimes we read just for information. You did this in the previous page when you answered questions about the information found on two different food labels. Another example is when we read a timetable or a map.

TOP TIP
Reading for information is a skill that you will use throughout your life, in many different situations. The more accurately you can read information, the easier many tasks will become. For example, if you read the set-up instructions for a new iPod accurately you will be able to finish the task much more quickly than if you just go ahead and try to programme it.

38

For example, we would read the London Underground map to find out how to get to different underground stations: which underground train line to take, where to change lines, how many stops we have to travel.

UNDERSTANDING *

BE ACTIVE

TASK 1

Using the internet, look at the London Underground map and research its history. Then write a short paragraph about your findings.

TASK 2

Working in small groups, look again at the London Underground map. Explain how the use of colour makes the map easier to read.

TASK 3

Imagine that you and a group of friends are going to London for the weekend. Using the Trainline website, plan the train journey from the station nearest to your home to London.

Write down the train times, any station changes that you have to make, and the time that you arrive in London.

TASK 4

You and your friends decide to stay in a hotel near Marble Arch underground station in London.

Using the London Underground map, write down the plan of the route by Underground from Kings Cross station to Marble Arch.

Then plan a route from Marble Arch underground station to Islington station, and from Islington station to Leicester Square. Then plan your route from Leicester Square back to Marble Arch.

Set out your route as effectively and clearly as you can so that it is easy to read at a later date.

READING FOR UNDERSTANDING

MAKE THE LINK

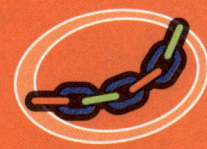

We learn map reading skills in **Geography**. We also learn about different places.

The London Underground map is a famous design. We learn more about design in **Art and Design**, and **Craft and Design**.

DID YOU KNOW?

The London Underground map is highly symbolic and doesn't represent the actual route of all underground lines. In addition, the stations have changed over the years, with many old stations now closed.

It is possible to glimpse these 'ghost' stations when travelling on the London underground, and they are sometimes used settings for novels and short stories.

In London, the underground is mostly referred to as the 'Tube'. However in Glasgow, underground trains are called the 'subway', which is the same name used by many other cities with underground train systems – New York, for example, calls its underground 'the subway'. In Paris, the underground train system is called the 'metro'.

OUR EVERYDAY LIVES:

In Scotland, Glasgow is the only city with an underground train system. Most other towns and cities have bus services as the main form of public transport, and publish details of bus routes and times so that people can plan their journeys. The London Underground map is so iconic in its design that it has influenced the design of bus route maps too.

READING ACCURATELY

It is easy to read what we think is there rather than what is actually there. This can be a real problem when it comes to tests and exams, as people can sometimes answer the question that they think is being asked instead of reading it accurately, which usually means lost marks.

TOP TIP
Make sure that you take your time and read as accurately as you can – especially when you are reading instructions.

EXAMPLE

Look quickly at the diagram below for just a few seconds and look away again. Now write down what you saw written within the triangle.

PARIS
IN THE
THE SPRING

Now look at what you have written – did you write 'Paris in the Spring'? If so, you have read the text in the triangle incorrectly – check it again! It's easy to write what you think.

40

UNDERSTANDING *

BE ACTIVE

Close reading passages are short passages which are often used to test the accuracy of your reading. Let's try one now. Read the passage below by Cate Devine:

> The first special constables to police Loch Lomond National Park, and the first of their kind in the UK, took up their truncheons yesterday to begin a 'daunting and exciting' new career in curbing anti-social behaviour at the world-famous beauty spot.
>
> On Loch Lomond itself, the only loch within the national park to have by-laws in place, inappropriate use of speedboats is the main problem. On the lochside the four new special constables will be responsible for policing wild camping, alcohol-fuelled breaches of the peace, assault, littering and vandalism such as using fences and rare trees for firewood.
>
> This groundbreaking partnership between the National Park Authority and Central Scotland Police was described yesterday as 'really exciting' by Fiona Logan, Chief Executive of the Loch Lomond and the Trossachs National Park Authority.
>
> 'We are proud to play our part in promoting safer communities and ensuring that all our visitors have a positive experience,' she said.

Now answer these questions.

1. In what two ways is the appointment of the special constables unique?
2. In your own words, say what the job of the special constables will involve.
3. What, according to the writer, is the main problem on Loch Lomond itself?
4. What is the Chief Executive's attitude to the partnership? Is he annoyed or pleased?

READING FOR UNDERSTANDING

MAKE THE LINK

We learn about places such as Loch Lomond in **Geography**.

We learn more about the natural environment in **Biology**.

We learn about responsible citizenship in **Social Education**.

DID YOU KNOW?

Loch Lomond is twenty-four miles long, five miles wide and is 600 feet deep. There are about thirty-eight islands. People live on some of the islands, and there is even a hotel on one!

Loch Lomond is one of the world's most famous lochs. The area is known for its beauty, which has inspired many writers to write songs and poems about it.

OUR EVERYDAY LIVES:

In our everyday lives, we are bombarded by reading material – newspapers and magazines, adverts on billboards and the sides of buses, signs in supermarkets and shopping centres.

We often tend either to ignore signs or not to read them accurately. In some cases, however, we do need to pay attention to the reading material that surrounds us – for example we need to read warning signs and instructions accurately.

MAKING INFERENCES FROM TEXTS

Sometimes the meaning of a text is **implied** rather than fully said. In this case, we have to **infer** ideas from a text.

The word **imply** means that the writer has not quite fully said something. The word **infer** means that the reader has to work out the idea from the text. In other words, the writer **implies** (something) and the reader **infers** (that same thing).

EXAMPLE

'Captain Ian Sercombe was frightened. He rested a broad forefinger on the control column of the Boeing 747 and eased back on his seat. Glancing out of the cabin windows at the sixty metres of his giant machine's wingspan, he tried to calm himself with thoughts of its size and detail…'

We can **infer** from this paragraph that something is going to go wrong with this flight – the plane's captain is 'frightened', he tries to 'calm himself' which **implies** that he is anxious about the plane.

TOP TIP
You should know the difference between infer and imply. Remember that the writer implies and the reader infers.

42

UNDERSTANDING *

BE ACTIVE

Here is some more of the short story.

'Decent night, Skip.'

First Officer, Les Bright's voice cut in on Ian's thoughts. The two men had completed the pre-take-off check and were sitting on the flight deck. Outside a huge moon hung in the hot tropical night sky which pressed down on Singapore's Changi airport.

Les Bright was talking to the control tower when Cabin Service Director Edwina Reeves came into the flight deck area.

'Two hundred and sixty passengers and thirteen cabin crew all safely aboard, Captain. Cabin secure.'

'Thanks, Edwina,' replied Ian. 'We should be off very soon.'

Minutes later, the huge aircraft began to roll away from its stand at the airport. The time was 8.04 p.m. and the journey to Perth, Australia, had begun.

QUICK TASK

To answer the following questions, you might need to infer information from the passage.

1. Is Les Bright as anxious as Captain Ian Sercombe? How do you know?
2. What words does the Cabin Service Director use that might have reassured the captain?
3. What do you think it is that's going to go wrong with the flight? Can you infer anything from the paragraph beginning 'First Officer, Les Bright's voice cut in...'?

READING FOR UNDERSTANDING

MAKE THE LINK

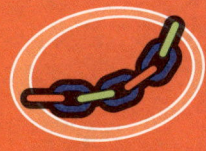

In **Geography**, we learn more about countries such as Singapore and Australia.

In **Physics** we learn about gravity, motion and force, which helps us to understand how aeroplanes can fly.

DID YOU KNOW?

The flight in the story is going to Australia. Australia is a large island which is geographically isolated (there are not any countries which are very close to it). This isolation means that Australia has animals that are only found there – kangaroos, koala bears, wombats and birds such as the emu and kookaburra. Australia also has more species of reptiles than any other country and a large number of poisonous snakes!

43

OUR EVERYDAY LIVES:

On some flights, especially from the west coast of the USA to Australia, you have to fly across the International Date Line. The International Date Line is an imaginary line on the surface of the earth where the date changes if you travel east or west across it – if you travel east you lose 24 hours; if you travel west you gain 24 hours.

So, for example, if you fly from San Francisco travelling west across the International Date Line, you gain a day – 24 hours.

COMPARING TEXTS

Learning objective: to be able to compare two texts by looking at purpose, structure, readership, and register.

EXAMPLE

Let's look at two newspaper headlines.

(a)

I GOT £50 FINE... FOR DROPPING A TENNER
Shopper Stewart busted by cops over litter rap

and

(b)

| 16 news | 12.04.2009 sundayherald |

Design flaws in nuclear transport ships increase the risk of accidents, claims report

Consultant says claims of safety 'lack scientific ...

MESSY BUSINESS
IT'S the world's dirtiest job, it costs at

Headline (a) is taken from a **tabloid** newspaper, from *The Sun* [11 June 2009].

Tabloid headlines have a structure and a style of their own. The shape and structure not only help us identify the text as a headline but both are intended to catch our eye and make us read on.

In (a), note the use of the word 'tenner' for 'ten pounds' or £10, and the word 'busted' – both are examples of informal language. Note also the repetition of the 's' sound in 'Shopper Stewart' (the repetition of a consonant is referred to as **alliteration** – an effect which is often used by tabloid newspapers).

Headline (b) is from the *Sunday Herald*, a **quality** newspaper. You can see right away that it is different. Its language is much more formal.

TOP TIP
Newspapers are known to sometimes present opinions as facts, or, worse, to present people or situations in the worst possible light in order to increase interest and therefore sales. Remember that not everything that appears in newspapers is necessarily true!

44

UNDERSTANDING *

BE ACTIVE

TASK 1

In your groups, answer the following questions:

1. What is the **purpose** of headline (a)? Is it to inform, to catch people's interest, to annoy, to get sympathy?
2. How is it **structured**? Is it a statement or a question?
3. Is it grammatically correct? How should it read if it were to be written formally? Who is the intended **reader**? A police officer, a bank manager, a delivery driver, a nurse?
4. What is the **register**? Is it formal, informal, serious, witty, angry, pleading? Give reasons for your answers.

TASK 2

In the same groups, what do you think is the purpose of headline (b)? To attract attention or to tell the reader about the content of the story? In structure it uses formal language. The subheading – 'Consultant says claims of safety "lack scientific and technical credibility"' – gives even more detail.

TASK 3

One member of the group should be prepared to give a talk to the whole class on the differences between these two headlines – but the talk should try to make comparisons point by point, rather than deal with one headline and then the other.

TASK 4

Bring to the classroom an example that is typical of tabloid newspaper headlines.

Be prepared to talk to your group about why you think it is typical.

MAKE THE LINK

You will study newspapers in **Modern Studies**. You may also look at old newspaper stories in **History**.

DID YOU KNOW?

There are two kinds of newspapers in the UK – **tabloid** newspapers and **quality** newspapers. The very names indicate the differences between the two. **Tabloid** papers are small in size, made for easy reading in public places. The pages can be turned without disturbing other people in small spaces, such as trains and buses. **Quality** papers are sometimes referred to as **broadsheet** newspapers, simply because they are bigger and printed on broad sheets. Recently, however, broadsheets are being printed on smaller paper, the same size as the tabloids, but to avoid confusion they are referred to as **compacts**.

45

OUR EVERYDAY LIVES:

Tabloid newspapers – *The Sun*, *The Daily Record*, *The Mirror* – tend to be cheap, and often print stories about the lifestyles of celebrities. Their headlines tend to be sensational and eyecatching.

Quality newspapers, on the other hand – *The Guardian*, *The Herald*, *The Scotsman*, *The Times* – tend to be more expensive, and are more concerned with news, analysis, comment, and politics. Their headlines tend to be more sober and serious to reflect the subject matter of the news story.

PERSUASION

It's important to be able to tell the difference between facts and opinions. Facts are indisputable and can be supported by evidence. For example, it is a fact that Edinburgh is the capital of Scotland.

However, it is a matter of opinion whether Edinburgh is the most beautiful city in Scotland. The trouble is that some opinions are made to look like facts.

EXAMPLE

For example, opinions are often made to look like facts in adverts. The slogan 'probably the best lager in the world' is an opinion, not a fact and the word 'probably' in the slogan makes this clear. However, what about the claim 'Active X is the best cleaner in the world'? That sounds like a fact, but how could it be proved? Which other cleaners is it better than? Where are the results to prove this? There aren't any, therefore it's an opinion which is used to persuade people to buy Active X.

An important reading skill is being able to distinguish between facts and opinions. For example, think about the statement 'the M8 is the motorway that goes from Glasgow to Edinburgh'. Is it unarguably true? To prove its truth, you can go and check – the M8 is the motorway between Edinburgh and Glasgow, so the statement is true.

Now take the statement that 'dark chocolate is tastier than milk chocolate'. Is that a fact or an opinion?

Ask yourself whether it is unarguably true – it's not, so the statement is an opinion.

TOP TIP
Next time you read an advert, check carefully whether claims that appear to be facts aren't really opinions.

46

UNDERSTANDING *

BE ACTIVE

TASK 1

In pairs, say whether the following statements are facts or opinions. In each case, ask yourselves if the statement is unarguably true.

- Inverness is the capital of the Highlands.
- The tallest mountain in the United Kingdom is Ben Nevis.
- Bananas are the tastiest food.
- Chocolate is bad for dogs.
- Gentlemen prefer blondes.
- Chicken Tikka is Scotland's favourite meal.

TASK 2

Quite often adverts make claims that appear to be facts but are really just opinions. Let's look at another label.

Chicken Passanda

Pieces of marinated chicken in a delicious mild creamy curry sauce.

The authentic taste of India.

500 g

Use by
09 JUN
Keep in fridge 2 to 5°C

Suitable for freezing

Approx. per pack
Cals 650
Fat 45g
Salt 2.8g

Mild

1. Look at the label. Working with a partner, decide which are facts and which are opinions.

2. Working with your partner, try to work out the justification for the claim that Chicken Passanda is 'the authentic taste of India'. What do you think the purpose of this claim is?

MAKE THE LINK

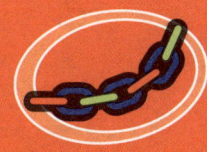

We learn about food labels in Home Economics.

We learn facts in **History**, but are sometimes asked to give an opinion on events – for example, it is a fact that Mary, Queen of Scots was queen of Scotland, but was she a good queen?

DID YOU KNOW?

Advertisers can only state facts if they are true – they cannot give false information. For example, chocolate bars cannot claim to help weight loss as this is obviously untrue!

This is why advertisers try to present opinions as facts – but they still have to word their statements in a way that makes it clear that it is an opinion being presented.

OUR EVERYDAY LIVES:

Adverts are a good example of texts that try to use persuasion – they want us to buy their products. Newspapers are another example as they often try to influence our opinions through persuasion. Being able to identify opinions and facts helps us to make our own minds up about things.

RELIABILITY

If something is in print, we tend to believe that it is true. In a sense, we have to since we don't have the time (or the energy!) to check on the truth of everything that we read.

But we should remember that everything is written in a context and that **context** can affect the viewpoint of the writer.

EXAMPLE

For example, what has been written of William Wallace (1270–1305) can vary from referring to him as the greatest national hero the Scots have ever had to calling him a traitor and a bloodthirsty terrorist. The view depends on the political background of the writer, but what is the truth? How reliable is the information we have of any historical figure? Historians try to read several accounts of an event or a person to try and get several viewpoints – this helps to give them a more balanced view.

48

Even newspapers aren't always reliable. They want to print stories that will sell, and sometimes truth is sacrificed in favour of selling more copies. They sometimes present opinions as facts or present people or situations in the worst possible light in order to increase interest and sales.

TOP TIP
Don't believe everything that you read in the papers!

UNDERSTANDING *

BE ACTIVE

By visiting the History Department, the library, and by searching the Internet, find out all you can about the Battle of Culloden (1746).

TASK 1

List 5 facts about the Battle.

TASK 2

List 5 opinions that a survivor of Bonnie Prince Charlie's army might have made about the Battle.

List 5 opinions that one of the Duke of Cumberland's supporters might have made after the defeat of the Prince's army.

TASK 3

You are a reporter for the BBC's Reporting Scotland, based in Glasgow. You have been sent by the programme's editor to Culloden to present a report on the outcome of the Battle.

Write out the text of your report, trying to be as unbiased as possible.

TASK 4

You are a reporter for the Highland Herald, based in Skye. You are a loyal supporter of the Jacobite uprising. You have witnessed the entire Battle from start to finish and you send in your report of all that happened.

Obviously, your report is biased towards the Highlanders, even although they were defeated. Your report obviously contains more opinion than fact, reflecting your own views of the event.

Write the article that appeared in the *Sunday Highland Herald* on the 17th April 1746.

READING FOR UNDERSTANDING

MAKE THE LINK

In **Modern Studies**, you learn about the political biases of newspapers and how this can affect the reliability of a newspaper story.

DID YOU KNOW?

Wikipedia is an online encyclopaedia that is used by millions of people around the world. It is unique in that it allows its users to write entries and edit entries that are already there.

Wikipedia's founders wanted to make knowledge accessible to everyone. Letting people write what they like, however, means that many entries on Wikipedia are inaccurate and unreliable.

If you use Wikipedia as a source of information, be sure to double-check its claims elsewhere too!

49

OUR EVERYDAY LIVES:

The internet is a brilliant source of information, which people are able to access easily through search engines such as Google. However, as Wikipedia shows, not all information found online is reliable. Health information in particular is often incorrect, such as a claim several years ago that using underarm deodorants can cause breast cancer. When you are searching for information online, always check that it is from a reliable source such as NHS Online and if you have any doubts about health information in particular, check again with your doctor.

INTRODUCTION

Learning objective: to understand how to go about analysing a text.

As well as reading for information – labels, instructions, dictionaries – we also read for pleasure. We watch television and films for the same reasons.

Asking questions

When reading a book for pleasure, we can ask ourselves three questions to help us understand why we enjoy it:

1. What is the text (novel, play, poem, film, soap opera) about?
2. What techniques have been used to tell us what it's about?
3. How do those techniques contribute to what it's about?

The answer to question 1 is **theme**: the text is about love or the triumph of good over evil or about a young person's experience of growing up. The theme always has something to do with the human condition – usually about our relationships with other people.

The answer to question 2 is about **technique** – structure, characterisation, establishing and developing setting. In other words, the way(s) in which a story is told – its plot.

The answer to question 3 concerns **textual analysis**. When it comes to writing about novels, plays, and poems, it is important to be able to understand and analyse the connection between the theme and how the theme is portrayed. Once you know how to do that, writing an essay about novels, plays and poems will become straightforward for you all the way through secondary school.

TOP TIP

Question 1 involves **understanding**, question 2 involves **analysis** and question 3 involves **analysis and evaluation**. The next time your teacher reads you a story or a poem, use the three questions to help form your response to it. If he/she asks what you think of the story, you now know that you can say 'Well, I think it's about fear'. In other words, you now know that your first job is to say what you think is the theme of the story or poem. Then you can go on to say something about the techniques used to help portray that theme.

EXAMPLE

Take the novel or short story (or drama text or poem) that you are studying in English at the moment. Now apply the three questions to it.

Question 1 What is its theme? Remember that a text can have more than one theme – and that the theme that you see in it may not be the same as the theme your partner sees in it – but that doesn't matter. What matters is that you are able to go to the text and find evidence that your theme is included in the text.

Question 2 Next you have to look at the various techniques which the author may well have used in order to portray the theme – structure, setting, characterisation, symbolism. All of these techniques will be discussed in detail later in this chapter.

Question 3 Finally, you have to ask yourself how – in what ways – the author has used these techniques to portray the theme.

These questions will be applied in more detail later in this chapter.

50

ENJOYMENT ⭑ READING

BE ACTIVE

TASK 1

Tonight, watch an episode of a TV soap – *Hollyoaks, Coronation Street, Eastenders, Neighbours, River City* – it doesn't matter which one.

Write down the name of the soap and beside it write down which theme(s) you think it is dealing with.

TASK 2

In your pairs, think of a theme for a short story – jealousy, revenge, greed, love, unrequited love (love which is not returned by the loved one), or any other theme that comes to mind.

Next invent two characters and a setting in time and place that would help portray that theme.

TASK 3

Make a list of your favourite novels, short stories, poems and plays and beside each title write down the theme(s).

Remember that there can be more than one theme.

READING FOR ENJOYMENT

MAKE THE LINK

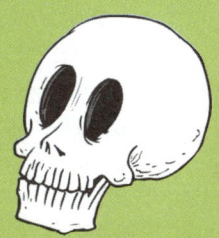

It's the same with television and film – all dramas explore a theme (or maybe more than one) and each is portrayed by various techniques – the difference is that in film and television the techniques involve close-ups, long shots, panning, fade-outs, which are all techniques to do with a visual medium.

In your **Drama** class, you also study plays – though more from the acting and production side. There you are interested in drama in performance. Part of a director's job is to make sure that the film or play makes the theme clear.

DID YOU KNOW?

It is impossible to have a story without a theme. Whether we are thinking of Shakespeare's *Hamlet* or last night's episode of *Hollyoaks*, there is always some issue or other being explored.

OUR EVERYDAY LIVES:

When next you pick up a book from the library or buy one from a bookshop, think about these three questions:

- What's the novel about?

- What techniques have been used to establish and develop the theme?

- How do those techniques contribute to the portrayal of the theme?

GENRE

Learning objective: to know what genre means and to be aware of different genres.

Genre is a French word which we use in English to mean type or kind. It's a way of classifying texts into:

- drama,
- prose,
- poetry.

Each of these genres can, of course, be further classified or subdivided. For example, prose can be subdivided into prose fiction (which involves novels and short stories) and prose non-fiction (which involves newspapers articles, essays, biographies, autobiographies and travel books).

Within prose fiction we can further subdivide novels into crime, horror, science fiction and so on.

The various genres, then – including drama, prose, poetry, television soaps, radio drama, films – are made up of stories, put together by one or more persons.

TOP TIP

Identify the genre first – drama, prose, poetry, film, television – before you try to identify the sub-genre.

52

EXAMPLE

Title	Genre	Sub-genre
Stig of the Dump by Clive King	Prose fiction	Adventure/fantasy
Stone Cold by Robert Swindells	Prose fiction	Murder/mystery/thriller
The Pied Piper of Hamelin by Robert Browning	Poetry	Narrative poem
Scotland's Story by Tom Steel	Prose non-fiction	History
Cider with Rosie by Laurie Lee	Prose non-fiction	Autobiography
Coronation Street	Television drama	Soap opera
A Christmas Carol by Charles Dickens (play version)	Drama	Ghost story
Mamma Mia directed by Phyllida Lloyd	Film	Musical comedy

ENJOYMENT ✴ READING

BE ACTIVE

QUICK TASK

Here are examples of sub-genre for poetry. Using the Internet and some of the poetry books in the library and the English Department, find two poems that belong to each of these sub-genre:

Type of Poem	Definition
Ballad	A narrative poem or song of popular origin, with a violent or supernatural theme, usually in short stanzas and often with a refrain (chorus).
Lyric	A short poem (usually) that expresses a powerful emotion or sentiment. Lyrics are the words of a song.
Sonnet	Poem of 14 (though sometimes 16) lines – often there are two stanzas where the rhyme of both stanzas is slightly different. Often there is a rhyming couplet at the end for dramatic effect.
Dramatic Monologue	Where a character speaks to a silent audience revealing aspects of his/her character as he/she does so.
Elegy	A serious poem, usually meant to express grief or sorrow. The theme is serious, usually death.
Haiku	Japanese poem in three lines of 5, 7, and 5 syllables, usually comical, incorporating a word or phrase that symbolises one of the seasons.

MAKE THE LINK

The idea of categorising literature, film, and television programmes is not new. Think of the various award ceremonies (BAFTAs, the Oscars, Golden Globes) – what genres and sub-genres do they use? See how many you can list.

DID YOU KNOW?

It's important not to use types of readership as the basis for identifying sub-genre: although there is children's fiction and young adult fiction, these are not really genres as such. It's better to identify sub-genre by content (Western, science-fiction, mystery, gothic).

53

OUR EVERYDAY LIVES:

It can be very difficult sometimes to distinguish between fiction and non-fiction. In a sense all fiction (novels and short stories) has to be based on the writer's experience, therefore must contain elements of non-fiction, and any non-fiction story, such as when you relate events that have happened to you, often contain an element of fiction – you sometimes invent bits to make your story more interesting. It is the same with authors.

THEME

As you already know by now, every story is about something; it makes some point or it explores some aspect of what it is to be human.

Stories can be about fear or greed or revenge or love or the triumph of good over evil. In other words, each story has to have a **theme**. If you think of last night's episode of Eastenders or Coronation Street or Hollyoaks, some issue or concern or theme that involves human beings would have been explored. Sometimes we also relate to or identify with the characters and/or the situation.

But in order to present and explore the theme, the writer or director (if it's television or film) has at his or her disposal certain techniques – such as making up characters, choosing settings or inventing the plot.

TOP TIP

When reading a play or novel or poem (or watching a film or television drama) try to identify the theme – what is the story about, what are its concerns, what issues is it exploring?

EXAMPLE

A director wants to make a film about fear. He chooses for his character a middle-aged woman who is returning alone from her holidays. Then he chooses for the setting an isolated house in the country, up a dark and lonely tree-lined path. He then chooses to set it at night, with only the moon to light the way. The taxi breaks down at the beginning of the path, and so the character has to walk all the way up it, as owls hoot and the moon disappears from time to time behind clouds.

In order to portray the theme of fear, the writer and director deliberately choose setting, character and plot to strengthen that theme.

54

ENJOYMENT ＊ READING

BE ACTIVE

TASK 1

You have already classified all the literature that you have studied in class into its genres. Now say what the themes of these various texts are.

TASK 2

At home, watch any of the soaps and in your groups the following day say what themes were being explored or dealt with.

TASK 3

What themes would you like some of these soaps to deal with? In your groups, give reasons for your choices.

TASK 4

Again, in groups, discuss the themes of the most recent films you have watched.

In your answers for Task 1, you listed the themes of all the literature that you have so far studied.

TASK 5

It is so important to be able to identify the theme of any text – whether the text be written or film or televisual. But it is just as important to be able to provide evidence from the text to support your idea of the theme.

For example, you might want to show how the setting and/or characterisation help convey the theme that you have identified.

Look at the example box on the opposite page and think again about what is said there. Now write down your opinion about how the director has used setting and characterisation to convey the theme of fear.

TASK 6

Now choose one of the texts you have listed for Task 1 and go on to write a short piece about how the writer has used setting and characterisation to convey the theme you have chosen.

READING FOR ENJOYMENT

MAKE THE LINK

Themes are portrayed by the plays and sketches that you are studying in **Drama**.

DID YOU KNOW?

The back cover of a book, especially a novel, often contains what is known as the 'blurb' – a summary of the plot along with a series of comments about the book by the publisher; sometimes there are also quotations from newspaper and magazine reviews of the book. It is here that reviewers will often say what they think the theme is. What is important to remember is that these are only opinions and that your opinion is just as valid. You may see different themes – and that is good, as long as you can justify them by reference to the text itself. You have to be able to go to the text to show where you are getting your ideas from – but those ideas are just as valid as anyone else's opinion.

OUR EVERYDAY LIVES:

We use the word 'theme' in non-literary contexts – we have theme parks, theme bars, theme restaurants. What exactly is a 'theme park' and in what way is the word 'theme' being used differently from the theme of a novel or play?

STRUCTURE: TIME

All fiction has to be structured in time. The novel or short story you are reading has to have a beginning, a middle, and an end. It might begin in the middle and go back in time so that the structure becomes middle>beginning>end, but the end always has to come at the end!

The structure middle>beginning>end is sometimes referred to as **flashback**, a technique often used in films.

Flashback lets the reader (or viewer) understand episodes that took place before the main event of the novel or film. Sometimes novels use mini flashbacks so that events that took place before the story began are explained to the reader. It's a technique that can help us to understand character.

TOP TIP

You can usually tell if a novel is structured using flashback because it will begin with the present tense then go into the past tense.

EXAMPLE

Perhaps one of the best examples of flashback is *Treasure Island* by Robert Louis Stevenson:

> Squire Trelawney, Dr. Livesey and the rest of the gentlemen having asked me to write down the whole particulars about Treasure island, from the beginning to the end, keeping nothing back but the bearings of the island, and that only because there is still treasure not yet lifted, I take up my pen in the year of grace 17 - , and go back to the time when my father kept the 'Admiral Benbow' inn, and the brown old seaman, with the sabre cut, first took up his lodging under our roof.
>
> I remember him as if it were yesterday, as he came plodding to the inn door, his sea-chest following behind him in a handbarrow; a tall, strong, heavy, nut-brown man; his tarry pigtail falling over the shoulders of his soiled blue coat; his hands ragged and scarred, with black, broken nails; and the sabre cut across one cheek, a dirty, livid white. I remember him looking round the cove and whistling to himself as he did so, and then breaking out in the old sea-song that he sang so often afterwards:-

Often the clue to the use of flashback is that the story begins using the present tense – as is the case with Treasure Island. Notice that the first paragraph is in the present tense: 'I take up my pen'... 'and go back to the time'

– a clear indication that flashback is going to be used, and the phrase 'go back in time' is actually mentioned, making the technique of flashback clear to the reader.

ENJOYMENT ★ READING

BE ACTIVE

TASK 1

Think again about the books you have read in class so far. Have many of them used the flashback technique?

TASK 2

Flashback technique is used a great deal in films and TV. In groups, make a list of five films and five television programmes that you know have used this technique. Do you think that the flashback technique was effective in each case? If so, as a group list your reasons why you think it was effective, if not, list your reasons why not.

TASK 3

Working in pairs, plan a personal experience essay that uses flashback to tell some of the story.

READING FOR ENJOYMENT

MAKE THE LINK

In **Drama**, look out for plays that use flashback.

DID YOU KNOW?

Many television series, including *River City*, use flashback at the beginning of the current episode to explain what has just gone before: often such a flashback starts 'Previously...'. But increasingly, a number of television drama series use flashback by fading into black and white or a single colour, to give the viewer information that explains what has just happened.

57

OUR EVERYDAY LIVES:

Audiences are increasingly able to recognise flashback, especially in film and television dramas. In novels, however, the use of flashback can be so subtle that sometimes we hardly recognise it – it can be used in conversation between characters when one of them relates an incident in the past to explain the current situation or another character's behaviour. Look out for this when you next read a novel.

STRUCTURE: POINT OF VIEW – FIRST PERSON NARRATOR

Learning objective: to understand what is meant by narrative technique, particularly what is meant by **Point of View**.

A very important aspect of structure is the way in which the story is told. This is known as the narrative technique, or Point of View.

There are various ways in which an author can tell (or narrate) a story.

In other words there are various points of view. The two most common are **first person narrator** and **third person narrator**.

Lets look at first person narrator to begin with.

When one of the characters in the story is the narrator, then we call that point of view **first person narration**.

EXAMPLE

In the opening extract from *Treasure Island*, on page 56, the story is being told by Jim Hawkins, the person who becomes the cabin boy on board the Hispaniola.

We know this because in the very first sentence the narrator says that 'Dr Livesey, and the rest of these gentlemen asked me' to write down the story and, later on, the narrator says 'I take up my pen', all of which indicate that a character in the novel is the narrator. It's later on that we learn that his name is Jim.

TOP TIP

Authors know that readers like to be able to identify with at least one of the characters in a novel or short story. Using first person narration usually means that the reader can even more easily identify with the person telling the story.

The advantage of first person narration is that the reader gets to know and usually like the narrator. And we get to know exactly what he/she is thinking because we are 'inside the narrator's head'. Everything is told from his or her point of view.

However, the narrator has to be present at all times or else he/she has to learn about important events from other people – often by a conversation that uses flashback – or from a newspaper, a telephone call, a text, or an email. This problem arises in *Treasure Island*: at one stage when they are on the island itself, Jim hands over the narration to

Dr Livesey simply because he is elsewhere on the island and therefore cannot narrate what happens.

The other problem is that we have to take the narrator's word for everything.

Always be aware that with first person narration you, the reader, have to take the narrator's word for what is happening. The view that the reader gets of the situation and other characters is the narrator's view.

ENJOYMENT ★ READING

BE ACTIVE

Now try it yourself. Using first person narration, write the opening paragraph of a story from the point of view of one of the characters. It's quite tricky because you, as the author, have to write as though you are that character.

Try to make the character as different as you can from yourself – but you can base him or her on someone you know.

TASK 1
Try writing the opening paragraph of a story from your mum's point of view.

TASK 2
Now try writing the opening paragraph of a story from the point of view of the school bully.

TASK 3
Write the same opening paragraph as Task 2, but this time from the point of view of the bully's victim.

TASK 4
Try writing the opening paragraph of a story from the point of view of a very sensitive ghost.

Now choose one of the above and continue with the story, bearing in mind the purpose (in this case, your theme), the structure, your reader, and the appropriate register.

READING FOR ENJOYMENT

MAKE THE LINK

In film and in television drama the camera can become the first person narrator. Have you come across a scene where the camera takes the place of one of the characters? Maybe there's a crime about to take place and the murderer is lurking outside the victim's house. Suddenly, in front of the camera, the branches of a bush begin to part and we see, by means of the camera, exactly what the murderer sees: the lighted window, the curtains drawn open, the victim alone. The camera is acting as the first person narrator.

You can have first person narration in drama – there can be a narrator who introduces each scene and/or the various characters.

DID YOU KNOW?

First person narrated stories almost always have to use flashback and usually have to depend on information coming to them from other sources – other characters, telephone calls, emails, newspapers. This is the only way that the character can know of something that takes place either before the novel began or about something that takes place when it is impossible for the narrator to have witnessed it.

OUR EVERYDAY LIVES:

This is exactly what happens in our everyday lives. How do you know what happened before you were born? Someone tells you, in a kind of reality flashback. Your dad or your grandmother tells you. How do you find out what has happened to one of your friends when you weren't present? You're told afterwards by phone or by email or in a conversation with that friend or with another person who was there. It's exactly the same with first person narration.

STRUCTURE: POINT OF VIEW – THIRD PERSON NARRATOR

Learning objective: to understand third person narration, with the focus on one of the characters as a way of narrating a story.

With this method of telling a story, the point of view is third person and the focus remains with one person. The story centres on one of the characters, though that character does not narrate the story. The effect is similar to first person narration in that we do not get to know what other people are thinking or feeling. Many short stories use this method to tell the story.

EXAMPLE

Read this extract from *A High Dive*, by LP Hartley.

The circus-manager was worried. Attendances had been falling off and such people as did come – children they were, mostly – sat about listlessly, munching sweets or sucking ices, sometimes talking to each other without so much as glancing at the show. Only the young or little girls, who came to see the ponies, betrayed any real interest. The clowns' jokes fell flat, for they were the kind of jokes that used to raise a laugh before 1939, after which critical date people's sense of humour seemed to have changed, along with many other things about them. The circus-manager had heard the word 'corny' flung about and didn't like it. What did they want? Something that was, in his opinion, sillier and more pointless than the old jokes; not a bull's-eye on the target of humour, but an outer or even a near-miss – something that brought in the element of futility and that could be laughed at as well as with: an intentional joke against the joker. The clowns were quick enough with their patter but it just didn't go down: there was too much sense in their nonsense for an up-to-date audience, too much articulateness. They would do better to talk gibberish, perhaps. Now they must change their style, and find out what really did make people laugh, if people could be made to; but he, the manager, was over fifty and never good himself at making jokes, even the old-fashioned kind.

TOP TIP

The narrator is the person telling the story – the 'voice' you hear as you read the story. In third person narration, the narrator rarely interrupts the narrative to tell us what he (or she) is thinking. In *A High Dive*, we can take the narrator's word for what is happening, simply because the main character is not telling the story. The opinion we have of the circus-manager or his wife or the high diver is not being affected by any other character, as it would be in first person narration. The reader is being given a much more objective view of everything.

Immediately, you can see that the story is going to concentrate on one of the characters – the circus-manager, and it focuses on him all the way through the story. The whole story is about his worries about fewer people visiting the circus.

60

ENJOYMENT ★ READING

BE ACTIVE

In pairs, read the extract below. The point of view is that of the main character, Connie – everything we know about is from her. The other character is called Charles, but we do not know what he is thinking or feeling. Now in pairs, rewrite the extract, this time from Charles' point of view.

There was the soft whisper of a foot on the kitchen linoleum. Connie's hands closed convulsively. The only thought that came to her now was that she must breathe quietly.

There was a grey glow somewhere. The figure in the kitchen was throwing a torch beam on the floor. Then it halted, waiting. He knew that she was hiding somewhere in the house.

He went almost soundlessly into the living room. She saw the glow of the light there. Back into the kitchen. She heard him moving quietly – listening – toward the door through which she had come only a few seconds before to use the telephone.

He came through that door, within three feet of her. But when he was fully through the doorway she was behind him. Again he flashed the light downwards. But he did not think to look behind him. By just so much she was saved for the moment.

In the greyish light reflected from the floor she recognised him.

He went into the dining room. He moved very quietly, but he bumped ever so slightly against a chair. The noise made her want to shriek. He was hunting her, and he knew that she was in the house, and he had to kill her. He had to get his loot and get away, and she must not be able to tell anything about him.

READING FOR ENJOYMENT

MAKE THE LINK

Mostly with film and television drama the camera is the third person narrator. It stands back and just records the story for the audience.

DID YOU KNOW?

There is a third method of narration. Sometimes writers use an omniscient narrator – a narrator who knows everything about everybody. Here, the point of view is the third person, but the narrator knows all there is to know about all the characters. The omniscient narrator also knows what is going on in all the settings of the story: he/she, for example, can tell us what is happening to a family in Carrbridge and their cousins in Coatbridge. So it's unlike third person narration with the focus on one character – the omniscient narrator can focus anywhere and on anyone he or she wants.

61

OUR EVERYDAY LIVES:

The omniscient narrator method of telling a story is not very common, and it tends to be used mostly in novels, especially those that are set in a large number of places and have a large number of characters. A shorter novel, dealing with a shorter time-span, tends to focus on one character.

But when you think about it, the news and all non-fiction tends to be from the point of view of the omniscient narrator. The newsreader, for example, is able to range over a number of scenes and at no time does he or she offer an opinion!

CHARACTERISATION

Learning objective: to analyse the ways in which a character is established by the writer.

Let's look at the opening of the first chapter of *Harry Potter and the Philosopher's Stone* by JK Rowling.

EXAMPLE

'Mr and Mrs Dursley, of number four, Privet Drive, were proud to say that they were perfectly normal, thank you very much. They were the last people you'd expect to be involved in anything strange or mysterious, because they just didn't hold with such nonsense.

Mr Dursley was the director of a firm called Grunnings, which made drills. He was a big, beefy man with hardly any neck, although he did have a very large moustache. Mrs Dursley was thin and blonde and had nearly twice the usual amount of neck, which came in very useful as she spent so much of her time craning over garden fences, spying on the neighbours. The Dursleys had a small son called Dudley and in their opinion there was no finer boy anywhere.

The Dursleys had everything they wanted, but they also had a secret, and their greatest fear was that somebody would discover it. They didn't think they could bear it if anyone found out about the Potters. Mrs Potter was Mrs Dursley's sister, but they hadn't met for several years; in fact, Mrs Dursley pretended she didn't have a sister, because her sister and her good-for-nothing husband were as unDursleyish as it was possible to be. The Dursleys shuddered to think what the neighbours would say if the Potters arrived in the street. The Dursleys knew that the Potters had a small son, too, but they had never even seen him. This boy was another good reason for keeping the Potters away; they didn't want Dudley mixing with a child like that.'

The reader is being introduced to the Dursleys. Look at the language used to describe them and where they live: The Dursleys 'were proud to say that they were perfectly normal' which suggests that they delighted in normality, conforming to what is expected of people who live in middle-class suburbia (you might have to find out what 'suburbia' means – it's a location but also a set of attitudes!).

Another phrase helps build up a picture of what they are like: 'they didn't hold with such nonsense' which suggests that they lacked imagination. They want and delight in a simple, straightforward, uncomplicated life.

ENJOYMENT * READING

BE ACTIVE

TASK 1

Working as a group, answer the following questions after you have re-read the passage from *Harry Potter and the Philosopher's Stone*.

1. List all the unattractive things said about both Mr and Mrs Dursley.
2. Agree among your group about what the list suggests about the Dursleys. What kind of family are they, do you think? Base your answer on the items in your list.
3. What does the word group 'there was no finer boy anywhere' suggest about the boy himself and about them as parents?
4. Is there anything good to say about the Dursleys?
5. If the Dursleys are conformist, suburban, narrow-minded, unimaginative, and they can't bear the Potters, what does that imply about the Potters?

TASK 2

Now it's your turn to create character. First of all, you are writing a novel based on your school and locality. You are about to introduce a new character – a very shy teenage boy of about your own age. He has come from a different part of the country (think about accent) and has just arrived at your school. He is painfully shy and awkward (think about the way he is dressed and the way he behaves). Using columns similar to the ones below, list the characteristics you would give him.

Character	Appearance	Behaviour	Language

READING FOR ENJOYMENT

MAKE THE LINK

The word 'character' can have different meanings, depending on context. In **ICT**, for example, the word 'character' means the letters, numbers and symbols on a keyboard. In **History**, we refer to historical figures as 'characters'. Mary, Queen of Scots, for example, is an important character from our history, as is Robert the Bruce.

The process of conveying characters in **Drama** and novels is called characterisation – the ways in which dramatists and novelists present characters.

DID YOU KNOW?

Some people get so confused about characters, especially in soaps, that they write to them as though they were real. Some people actually send hate-mail to the villain of the soap, obviously not realising that the character is 'pretend' and is, in fact, being played by an actor.

OUR EVERYDAY LIVES:

There is a difference between a character in a novel or short story and a character in a film, television drama or a play in performance. In the novel and the short story the character does exactly what the writer tells him or her to do. In film, television drama, and plays an actor helps to present the character. Of course there are lines set down by the writer for the actor to speak, but the actor also adds his or her interpretation to those lines, using acting techniques and gestures, creating another 'layer' to the way we as the audience see the character. That's why, when we see a film of a book, we sometimes say ' but that's not how I imagined that character in the book'.

SETTING

Learning objective: to understand the importance of setting and its contribution to plot and the overall theme.

All novels, short stories, and plays have to be set somewhere. And what people tend to forget is that the setting involves not only **place** but also **time**. It is usually easy enough to identify where a novel or short story is set, but we may have to do some detective work to find out when it is set.

Let's look at some passages from *The Natives are Hostile*, a short story by Alastair Scobie.

EXAMPLE

Githogo, the Mau Mau[1] general, stepped out of the forest. He was a tall man, dressed in tattered shorts and a greatcoat. His feet were bare. He wore field glasses slung round his neck. He could not use them because he did not understand how they focused. They had been taken from Bwana[2] McDuffy, an eighty-year-old farmer the gang had slashed to pieces the month previously.

Marumbi, his right-hand man, came up to him, gesturing towards a clump of bushes. "We have the houseboy," he said. "His name is Kahera. He says the Memsahib[3] and the toto[4] are alone in the house. There is only the cook-boy, Kenanjui, a kitchen toto and Kahera in the house with them."

For a moment Githogo thought things over. The farmhouse lay in the evening light, a grey house built of cedar off-cuts; that is, the outside of the trunk that is stripped off at the sawmills in the high forests where the great trees are cut for pencil slats. By the grey house a woman played with a child. A woman in a blue dress, a child in a white dress.

NOTES

1. 'Mau Mau' was the name given to a group of Kenyan rebels, who wanted to end British Colonial rule.
2. 'Bwana' is a Swahili word meaning 'master'.
3. 'Memsahib' was a term of respect, used during the colonial period, for a European woman.
4. The 'toto' is the woman's child.

The presence of a Mau Mau gang lets us know that this story is set in Kenya, East Africa, sometime during the 1950s when the Mau Mau uprising was at its height. We also know that it is set near a forest: 'Githogo, the Mau Mau general, stepped out of the forest'.

The narrator mentions that 'a woman played with a child', and although that sounds like characterisation, the fact that it is a woman and a child suggests vulnerability. But there's more: note that the 'woman (is) in a blue dress, a child in a white dress', the colours suggest vulnerability and innocence. The place, then, is easy prey.

TOP TIP

Human beings like symbols: for example, we use red roses and a red heart to symbolise love, lilies to symbolise peace, the colour green to symbolise safety and care for the environment, yellow to symbolise sickness (it's the colour of the skin and eyes when a patient is ill with jaundice), cowardice, but also sunshine and happiness. Writers are aware of these symbols and make use of them for what they can suggest to a reader.

64

ENJOYMENT * READING

BE ACTIVE

Let's think a bit more about symbols.

TASK 1
Find out what the following colours are used to symbolise:

- **blue**,
- **red**,
- **brown**,
- **black**.

TASK 2
Certain fruits are also used symbolically. What's the symbolic significance of an apple?

TASK 3
In a film, if you see vultures circling overhead, what might they symbolise?

TASK 4
You and your partner have decided to make a serious film about ghosts and scary happenings. Think about the opening sequences of the film and the ways that the setting you choose and the weather will suggest to the audience what the film is going to be about. You are using the weather and the setting *symbolically*.

TASK 5
You and your partner are going to create a bad guy for a television police series. How would you dress him? What age would you make him? What name would you give him?

READING FOR ENJOYMENT

MAKE THE LINK

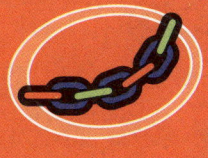

Symbols are also used in some of your other subjects:
Chemistry, for example, uses symbols for chemicals. These symbols make it easier for people of all nationalities to recognise chemical elements. The symbol H represents hydrogen and the symbol O represents oxygen and these two symbols are used to represent the chemical reaction involved when water is made: $H_2 + O_2 \rightarrow H_2O$.

But symbols are also used to represent hazardous waste. For example, what do you think this symbol indicates, especially by the use of the skull and crossbones?

DID YOU KNOW?

Setting can sometimes be a character in a novel or short story, helping to establish mood. Weather can also be part of setting and it, too, can contribute to the mood of a story. In film, sad scenes often take place in the rain – the rain not only contributes to the mood of the scene but symbolises the sadness of the characters and their situation.

OUR EVERYDAY LIVES:

We use symbols in our everyday lives. Symbols can be easier than words to understand quickly. Not only that but symbols are international – we don't need to know the local language if we can recognise the symbol.

What symbols do we use for:
- toilets,
- a level crossing,
- a battlefield,
- the stop sign at crossroads,
- something so dangerous that it could kill,
- the London Underground,
- your school.

PLOT

Learning objective: let's make a distinction between **narrative** and **plot**. A **narrative** is a series of events in a time sequence. For example, a narrative you hear in the news is a series of events in time – one event takes place and then another event follows it, then another, and so on.

Although **plot** is also a series of events in time sequence, there also has to be some *causal connection* between the events, and the cause (whatever it is) is usually connected with character.

Here is an example that is often used to explain the difference between a series of events and a plot.

The king died and then the queen died – series of events.

The king died and then the queen died of grief – plot.

The second example is plot because it includes a cause – the queen died because the king died and, obviously, the grief she felt for her husband's death overwhelmed her.

66

EXAMPLE

Let's take an example.

Mother shouts for boy to get up, his breakfast is ready. Boy gets out of bed, comes downstairs, walks into the kitchen, sees the toast, walks out again.

All of that is a narrative, nothing more – and it is told in a time sequence.

Now let's make the narrative into a plot.

Mother shouts *impatiently* for boy to get up, his breakfast is ready *and she is really fed up waiting for him*. Boy *eventually* gets out of bed, comes *angrily* downstairs, walks *sullenly* into the kitchen, looks *with contempt* at the toast, walks out again, *annoyed and resentful*.

We have now related these events to character and shown how one event causes another. We now know how the mother shouted for the boy, but we also want to know why? We also know how he reacted, but why did he react that way? What happened before this scene took place, and what is going to happen next? That's the way plot works – it arouses our curiosity. After all, much of the time we want to read on to find out what happens next.

Plot involves cause, character and emotion and they are all usually related to each other.

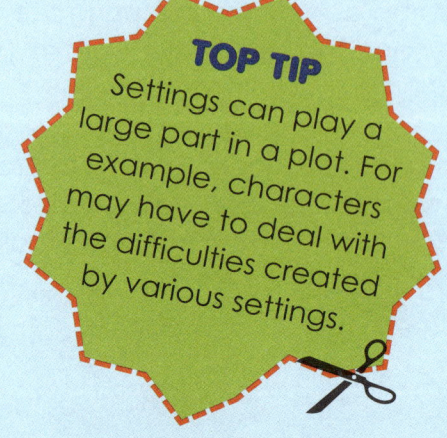

TOP TIP
Settings can play a large part in a plot. For example, characters may have to deal with the difficulties created by various settings.

ENJOYMENT * READING

BE ACTIVE

TASK 1

In your groups, discuss and write down the number of different ways in which we use the word 'plot'. When it comes to novels, short stories, and plays, however, we use the word 'plot' in a technical way. What is its technical meaning when used about literary texts?

TASK 2

For this activity, work in groups. We sometimes talk about the plot of a novel or drama being 'driven' and it can be driven by a character or, possibly more likely, an object. Decide among yourself which novel, play or film you all know where the plot is driven by an object. Maybe the object has special powers. Once you have decided, then note the ways in which the object helps 'drive' the plot.

TASK 3

In pairs, show what the plot devices are in *Treasure Island* or any other such book (any in the *Harry Potter series*, for example) that you both know well.

TASK 4

In pairs, find out what is meant by 'sub-plot'. Give an example from your own experience of a sub-plot – from a play you know, or a novel, or a television drama. Even dramas such as *River City* often employ sub-plots. Decide between you the advantages of a sub-plot.

TASK 5

Write out the opening paragraph of the story outlined above about the boy and his mother. Make sure that you include all that you have learned about plot.

READING FOR ENJOYMENT

MAKE THE LINK

Plot in drama tends to follow a pattern, almost a formula. At the beginning of a film or television drama, for example, everything can seem stable enough – but then something happens or another character arrives on the scene and everything changes. We say that the event or the new character acts like a catalyst – because the event or the character speeds up the reaction or the plot.

In science, too, particularly in **Chemistry**, you learn about **catalysts** – chemicals that speed up reactions.

DID YOU KNOW?

67

'Story' is one of those **portmanteau** words (a word that combines the meaning of two other words) that covers both narrative and plot. For example, when talking about news items we are most likely to use the word 'story' but we also say that the story in *Hollyoaks* at the moment is quite gripping.

OUR EVERYDAY LIVES:

It's important to remember that in our everyday lives when we read a novel or watch a film, one of the most important ingredients can be plot – that's what keeps us reading or watching. We want to find out what happens next. It's as simple as that. But of course, if we care for one of the characters, then we care about what happens to him or her, so characterisation comes into it.

PERSONAL RESPONSE TO READING

It's also important to be able to respond to the texts you have read and to be able to make some kind of personal comment on them.

Once you develop skills at examining how a writer (or a director of film or television drama) achieves his or her effect, you enjoy books and films even more.

TOP TIP
The great thing about enjoying reading is that it can have very practical uses. Never again will you be bored! Whenever you have to pass time waiting – as a passenger in a car, waiting at an airport, or travelling on a train or bus journey – if you have a novel you enjoy, then the time passes very pleasantly!

EXAMPLE

You have probably watched DVDs of your favourite films with friends or family. Have you then talked about the films afterwards? You might even disagree amongst yourselves whether or not it was good/gripping/amusing/entertaining. You might even talk about what you thought it was about – its themes. You might be able to see more than one theme in it – that the film or television drama is covering a number of related themes. But that's what it's all about – and that kind of discussion helps you make up your mind.

It's the same with reading. It can be fascinating discussing a book with like-minded people and these types of discussions help you learn to voice your opinion with confidence.

ENJOYMENT * READING

BE ACTIVE

Working in pairs, read this paragraph from *Through the Tunnel*, by Doris Lessing.

> Going to the shore on the first morning of the holiday, the young English boy stopped at a turning of the path and looked down at a wild and rocky bay, and then over to the crowded beach he knew so well from other years. His mother walked on in front of him, carrying a bright-striped bag in one hand. Her other arm, swinging loose, was very white in the sun. The boy watched that white, naked arm, and turned his eyes, which had a frown behind them, towards the bay and back again to his mother. When she felt he was not with her, she swung round. 'Oh, there you are, Jerry!' she said. She looked impatient, then smiled. 'Why, darling, would you rather not come with me? Would you rather…' She frowned, conscientiously worrying over what amusements he might secretly be longing for which she had been too busy or too careless to imagine. He was very familiar with that anxious, apologetic smile. Contrition sent him running after her. And yet, as he ran, he looked back over his shoulder at the wild bay; and all morning, as he played on the safe beach, he was thinking of it.

Now together answer the following questions.

(a) What **two expressions** tell the reader that Jerry and his mother had just newly arrived on holiday?

(b) Quote **two expression**s which indicate that Jerry's mother is concerned about him.

(c) Say in your own words what you think his mother is concerned about.

(d) From your reading of the paragraph, what do you think is likely to happen? Would you be likely to want to read on? If so, why, and, if not, why not?

READING FOR ENJOYMENT

MAKE THE LINK

Books are the source of so much of our knowledge and our wisdom. You have textbooks for **Maths** and some of your other subjects. But related to reading those textbooks is note taking. The act of writing helps us to remember information and note-taking can be an important part of the learning process.

DID YOU KNOW?

Books are now more popular than ever. Look at the increase in the number of bookshops in the High Street and shopping centres. And they are very attractively laid out – try to get into the habit of browsing round them. It's a very pleasant way of spending some time.

69

OUR EVERYDAY LIVES:

Make books and reading a part of your everyday life. Try to read different types of books by different authors. Many websites recommend books for young people and librarians and booksellers can also suggest different books that you might like to try.

GROUP DISCUSSIONS

Your teacher will from time to time set up group discussions and may ask one of you to be chairperson – someone to lead and control the discussion. When this happens, you have the chance to practise your listening and talking skills.

Your teacher will be looking for you to:

- listen carefully to what others are saying,
- think about what is being said,
- support what others are saying and/or challenge what others are saying,
- give your own views on the chosen subject.

70

EXAMPLE

If your teacher asks you to be the chairperson for a group discussion, there are some additional skills to practise. You need to be able to:

- control the discussion by making sure that everyone in the group has a chance to speak;
- encourage others to have their say or to expand on what they are saying;
- summarise the discussion to the rest of the class, so that you give a short, accurate account of what you talked about and what your group's main ideas and opinions were.

In other words, you have to be confident and responsible.

TOP TIP
People often use the term 'listen carefully' which suggests that to listen properly requires care, attention and skill.

LISTENING AND TALKING

BE ACTIVE

TASK 1

Form groups of four or five and hold a fifteen-minute discussion on a book that you are reading in English.

First of all, appoint a chairperson who will ensure that everyone gets a chance to speak. In turn, each of you should say what you think the main themes of the book are, whether or not you are enjoying it and why, and whether you read other books by the same author or which have a similar theme.

Make sure that everyone in the group has the chance to speak.

TASK 2

In groups of four or five, discuss ideas for writing a poem about the environment.

First appoint a chairperson who will make sure that everyone has the chance to share his/her ideas and who notes the ideas and decisions of your group. Discuss ideas for the poem, and then as a group try to write it.

TASK 3

Still in groups of four of five discuss your favourite school subjects. Each person should explain what their favourite subject is and why – what it is about that subject that interest them.

Make sure that everyone in the group has the chance to speak.

TOOLS FOR LISTENING AND TALKING

MAKE THE LINK

You may be asked to hold group discussions or to work in groups in other subjects. When this happens, you should always try to contribute your knowledge, ideas and opinions to the group and listen to what other people in the group say. **Social Education** in particular helps us to build confidence in taking part in group discussions.

Not only will you probably have group discussions all the way through school, almost every English class can be a group discussion, when the whole class can take place in discussing a poem, a play or a section from a novel.

DID YOU KNOW?

Group discussions aren't always face-to-face – social networking sites such as Facebook often host group discussions that people from all over the world can take part in.

The group discussion skills that you learn in school can be used when you join an online group discussion.

OUR EVERYDAY LIVES:

Many workplaces expect their employees to work in teams, therefore being able to communicate well in a group is an important skill. Employers try to hire people who listen carefully to others and consider their opinions and who can contribute their own ideas confidently as these are key skills for a good teamworker.

NOTE TAKING

Learning objective: to learn to take notes which can help you to plan an essay or take part in a group or individual discussion.

Note taking is an important skill for planning essays, group discussions and individual talks. Let's look first at note taking for an essay, then on the next page we will look at how to use these note taking skills for a group discussion.

Let's say you have to write an essay about someone you know – your grandmother or other older relative or even an older friend of the family. You need first of all to prepare a list of questions, then do the interview – once you know when the person was born, you can then do some research into what was happening, locally, nationally or even internationally at that time – this will give your essay some background. As you interview take notes, perhaps noting each stage in

that person's life – education, career, marriage and children. But also use your questions to find out what kind of person he/she is; try to convey his/her attitudes to things and people, what life was like when he/she was young. Try to work out the stages in that person's life.

TOP TIP

Notes should not be in formal English – you don't need to write in sentences – and you can use the dash instead of the full stop. The notes are a way of reminding you later of (in this case) the discussion that took place during the interview. The notes will help you write the biographical essay. The notes are not the plan – that comes later – but they will help you once you come to plan the way you are going to present the person's biography.

LISTENING AND TALKING

BE ACTIVE

TASK 1

Write an essay on whether or not the moon landing in 1969 actually took place. Investigate whether, perhaps, it was a conspiracy staged by the National Aeronautics and Space Administration (NASA), an agency of the United States government, in order to meet President Kennedy's promise of having a man on the moon before the 1960s ended.

Find out what evidence there is for such a conspiracy theory – that the whole thing took place in the Nevada desert – and what evidence there is that it did actually take place on the moon.

TASK 2

Working in pairs, research the best possible value for money mobile phone deal for someone of your age. You could do the research separately, then come together with your notes to put together your recommendations in a written report.

TASK 3

For this next task you need to work in groups. You are members of the planning committee of your local council and you have been approached by the Leader of the Council to present a report making recommendations about a suitable site for new age travellers who want to set up temporary residence near your town.

You have to find out about what they need as well as what services and resources are available, such as land, accessibility, water, sewerage, schooling, health, etcetera.

TOOLS FOR LISTENING AND TALKING

MAKE THE LINK

Note taking is a very useful skill; recognising what is important and noting it, while being able to recognise what is less important and ignoring it. Note taking is incredibly useful when revising for exams – in all subjects.

Taking notes provides material for you to study at a later date, and the very act of note taking can help you remember things – for example words in a foreign language.

DID YOU KNOW?

At one time there used to be a kind of written language called shorthand: it was a series of symbols and marks (which looked almost like hieroglyphics) which represented words. People trained in shorthand were able to take notes very quickly.

Shorthand fell out of use with the invention of small hand-held tape recorders.

OUR EVERYDAY LIVES:

The arrival of the PC and recording machines has removed the need for shorthand or even much note taking. Students at university lectures had to learn to be able to take notes as they listened to their lecturers, but much of that has been replaced by the hand-out – notes given out by the lecturer. But being able to take notes is still an important skill for some people – and can be if you want to write an essay that requires some research, where you have to find information from books, the internet, or other sources. Once you have located these sources you then have to take notes which will form the basis for your essay.

PREPARING FOR GROUP DISCUSSIONS

Group discussions are a great way to practise and develop both your listening and your talking skills. However these can be difficult to prepare for because you don't always know what the group discussion will be about.

Sometimes you may have a group discussion after you have studied a particular topic or issue – you then go into groups and discuss it. You may also go into groups to discuss a text that you are studying – for example, maybe you have just read a short story and you have to go into groups to discuss what you think it is about, or how the writer has established the setting.

One way to prepare for a group discussion is to make notes about the text or topic you are studying as you go along. Then you will remember your own ideas and opinions on the text or topic, and have something ready to discuss.

EXAMPLE

For example, the teacher reads you *The Monkey's Paw*, by WW Jacobs. You like it because its Gothic horror appeals to you. You are given a photocopy of the story, upon which you are allowed to make your notes.

Here's an example of the kind of notes you might make.

Sets atmosphere – wintry, miserable

WITHOUT, the night was cold and wet, but in the small parlour of Laburnam Villa the blinds were drawn and the fire burned brightly. Father and son were at chess, — cosy, relaxed, family-like the former, who possessed ideas about the game involving radical changes, putting his king into such sharp and unnecessary perils that it even provoked comment from the white-haired old lady knitting placidly by the fire.

Contrast – interior warm and snug.

reminder of outside/winter/stormy

"Hark at the wind," said Mr. White, who, having seen a fatal mistake after it was too late, was amiably desirous of preventing his son from seeing it. — suggestion of deviousness

foreshadowing / not everything is perfect.

"I'm listening," said the latter, grimly surveying the board as he stretched out his hand. "Check."

"I should hardly think that he'd come to-night," said his father, with his hand poised over the board.

Who is 'he'? curiosity built-up.

"Mate," replied the son.

"That's the worst of living so far out," bawled Mr. White, with sudden and unlooked-for violence; "of all the beastly, slushy, out-of-the-way places to live in, this is the worst. Pathway's a bog, and the road's a torrent. I don't know what people are thinking about. I suppose because only two houses on the road are let, they think it doesn't matter."

isolation established

suggestion of trouble

poor conditions of setting established

"Never mind, dear," said his wife soothingly; "perhaps you'll win the next one."

indication of wife's sharpness

LISTENING AND TALKING

BE ACTIVE

QUICK TASK

In groups, everyone should pick a television programme to watch. Make sure that everyone in the group watches a different programme.

Next day in your groups each member should present, in no more than a couple of minutes, the reasons why his or her programme is worth watching. Other members of the group must listen carefully, then offer opinions about the programme – and so on, round all the members of the group.

The same kind of group discussion can take place about favourite hobbies and sports, or about films and books.

These kind of group discussions should not be confused with individual talks. It isn't the case that one of you presents your favourite book or TV programme and then the group goes on to listen to the next presentation. This is a group *discussion*: each member has to *listen* to the *brief* talk, then you have to enter into a proper *discussion*, each one of you putting forward your ideas about what has just been said. It could be someone is talking about a comedy show on BBC Three: you have to respond to what has been said, give your opinion about the show and maybe about comedy shows in general – then the next person has to respond to what you have just said.

TOOLS FOR LISTENING AND TALKING

MAKE THE LINK

Being able to make notes on what you have read is a key skill for all of your subjects. It helps you to remember new information and leaves you prepared to discuss what you have learnt.

DID YOU KNOW?

Students preparing for exams at both school and university often make their own notes from class materials to help them revise.

Writing the information down again in their own words helps them to remember and understand it, and they can remind themselves of the key points by reading back through their notes in the weeks before the exam.

75

OUR EVERYDAY LIVES:

Group discussions take place every day both inside and outside of school – you may do a formal one on a set topic during your English class, then have an informal group discussion with your friends about a film during lunchtime, and a family discussion about your day when you get home from school. You can't always prepare for group discussions, especially when they are informal, but you can always contribute your knowledge, ideas and opinions.

PREPARING FOR AN INDIVIDUAL TALK

When preparing for an individual talk, you first need to choose a subject. Your teacher may give you a topic but if you are able to choose one for yourself try to choose something that interests you – a hobby, for example, or something that you have experienced or a television programme, film or book that you have enjoyed.

Once you have chosen a subject, you then have to decide the purpose of your talk. Is it to inform, entertain, persuade? You have then to do some research on your topic, so that you learn more about it and feel comfortable talking about it to others. Add in your own ideas and opinions, which will make your talk more interesting.

The next stage is to write down the points that you want to use in your talk. They then need to be organised – structured – according to purpose and audience.

For example, the audience may be your classmates and if part of your purpose is to entertain your classmates, then you have to structure your talk with that audience in mind. The fact that you want to entertain them will also decide the register you are going to use.

A talk sounds better if it is not read aloud from your notes. Some people, however, find that it's useful to make brief notes on their talk to help remind them of the points they want to make, and when in their talk they should make them. One way to make notes is to write them on index cards.

LISTENING AND TALKING

BE ACTIVE

TASK 1

Make a list of topics that interest you that you might like to give a presentation on.

TASK 2

Pick one topic from the list and write down what the purpose of your talk would be, e.g. is it to inform, entertain, or present your own opinion on an issue? how you would write (structure) it, who your audience would be and which register you would use.

TASK 3

Do the same two exercises again, but work with a partner. Decide together which topic you would both like to present then decide on purpose, structure, audience and register.

TASK 4

Now decide how you would present the talk to your class – who would present each part of the talk? Would you take it in turns, or would one of you introduce the other or sum up what your partner said?

Plan how you would present a joint talk.

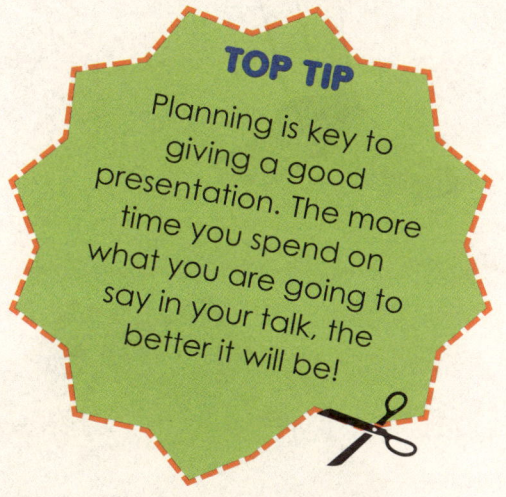

TOP TIP

Planning is key to giving a good presentation. The more time you spend on what you are going to say in your talk, the better it will be!

TOOLS FOR LISTENING AND TALKING

MAKE THE LINK

You may be asked to give an individual talk in other subjects. For example, in **RME** you may be asked to give your own views or opinions on a subject. In **History**, you may have to give a talk on a subject that you have studied. In **Modern Languages**, such as French or Spanish, you may be asked to give a talk in the language you are learning.

DID YOU KNOW?

Some people become very anxious about speaking in front of other people. Very occasionally it can turn into a phobia – a deep fear. Extreme fear of public speaking is known as **glossophobia**.

The word glossophobia comes from two Greek words: 'glossa' meaning tongue and 'phobos' meaning dread.

OUR EVERYDAY LIVES:

Talks don't end when you leave school. There are all kinds of occasions when you may have to talk in front of a group of people – for example, at a job interview or in front of workmates or as best man at a wedding.

Many people find it awkward to speak in public – so you must take the opportunities you are given at school to practise it. Not only that, but many job interviews nowadays involve giving a presentation – using a tool such as PowerPoint, for example – where you really do have to be able to be confident and engage the interviewers with body language and eye contact.

PRESENTING AN INDIVIDUAL TALK

When giving a talk try to:

Introduce your subject confidently. The introduction is where you capture your audience's interest – so you have to persuade them that you are worth listening to.

Pay attention to, even rehearse, your body language: Walk to the front confidently (even if you are nervous!), look up at the class, smile, and continue to look round the class, as though you are speaking to individual members of the class. If your talk is witty, watch the timing of your lines and allow for laughter – don't talk through it so that the audience misses the next point. Use open hand gestures to include your audience (a closed gesture is when you cover or block your body from the audience).

Project your voice. Make sure that you can be heard, especially by the people at the back of the room. Watch your teachers – they are all experts at projecting their voices right to the back of the classroom.

Present your ideas in a logical sequence, using linking words and phrases such as: however, not only... but also, although x was the case... y was also the case, on the other hand.

Try to avoid hesitation – don't keep saying 'um', 'er', 'eh'.

Use your conclusion to sum up what you have been saying. And signal that you are about to summarise your talk by using terms such as 'clearly', 'then', or even 'finally'.

REMEMBER!

Remember that your talk has to have a purpose or point – you can't just ramble on for four or five minutes! It has to have a structure, which is decided by the purpose – for example, an explanatory talk will be differently structured from a humorous one. But all talks will have an introduction, a middle, and a conclusion. The one aspect that's slightly different from the aspects of writing is that here you have an audience rather than a reader – but you must pay attention to that audience and be alert to its reaction. Then there is register – you have to word your talk in a way that makes sense to the audience.

TOP TIP
If you have used research, then use it to support your argument, and if your talk is from personal experience then make sure you use interesting detail to captivate your audience.

LISTENING AND TALKING

BE ACTIVE

QUICK TASK

An excellent way of developing your speaking skills is to play BBC Radio 4's game *Just a Minute*, which the whole class can play. Your teacher will select a subject, say, school uniform – although it could be something like such as *Dancing on Ice* or internet safety.

The teacher will choose one of you to speak, and you then have one minute in which to talk about the chosen subject. But, you are not allowed to hesitate, or repeat a word other than the words in the title. So if you are given school uniform as a subject, you must talk about it without repeating words such as 'blazer', 'shirt', 'tie', 'pupil'. You can repeat words such as 'the' or 'a' and 'an', but not any nouns or verbs.

If you pause to think, it's called 'hesitation'. If you say 'eh' or 'um', that too is counted as hesitation.

Your teacher will time the minute you have. Should you complete the minute without hesitation or repetition (a difficult task!), then you score one point. If someone successfully challenges you for hesitating, or repeating a word, then that person scores one point and takes up the subject for the time remaining, unless he or she is successfully challenged. The person who challenges towards the end of the minute (with, say, ten seconds to go) is likely to score one point for a successful challenge and one point for finishing the minute.

Playing *Just a Minute* will sharpen your listening skills and develop your talking skills.

TOOLS FOR LISTENING AND TALKING

MAKE THE LINK

We learn about projecting our voices and appearing confident even when we're not in **Drama**.

In **ICT** we learn how to use presentation software, such as PowerPoint, which can be used in presentations.

Social Education teaches us about the importance of good communication.

DID YOU KNOW?

Being able to speak well in front of groups of people is such an important life skill that there are many courses available to help people build their confidence in speaking.

Being able to communicate well with other people and being able to present your own ideas and opinions clearly is another important life skill – and there are also lots of courses to help people improve their communication.

OUR EVERYDAY LIVES:

Some people make a career out of being good speakers – they speak clearly and well, are able to speak in a way relevant to their audience and are confident speaking in front of other people.

Your teacher is one of these people!